I0066057

ADVANCES IN HUMAN AND MACHINE NAVIGATION SYSTEMS

Edited by **Rastislav Róka**

Advances in Human and Machine Navigation Systems
http://dx.doi.org/10.5772/intechopen.75272
Edited by Rastislav Róka

Contributors

Tamilselvam Nallusamy, Prasanalakshmi Balaji, Anuar Mohamed Kassim, Yasuno Takashi, Hiroshi Suzuki, Mohd Shahrieel Mohd Aras, Ahmad Zaki Hj. Shukor, Hazriq Izzuan Jaafar, Fairul Azni Jafar, Lianwu Guan, Xu Xu, Yanbin Gao, Hanxiao Rong, Meng Wang, Aboelmagd Noureldin, Kayoko Yamamoto, Rastislav Róka

© The Editor(s) and the Author(s) 2019
The rights of the editor(s) and the author(s) have been asserted in accordance with the Copyright, Designs and Patents Act 1988. All rights to the book as a whole are reserved by INTECHOPEN LIMITED. The book as a whole (compilation) cannot be reproduced, distributed or used for commercial or non-commercial purposes without INTECHOPEN LIMITED's written permission. Enquiries concerning the use of the book should be directed to INTECHOPEN LIMITED rights and permissions department (permissions@intechopen.com).
Violations are liable to prosecution under the governing Copyright Law.

(cc) BY

Individual chapters of this publication are distributed under the terms of the Creative Commons Attribution 3.0 Unported License which permits commercial use, distribution and reproduction of the individual chapters, provided the original author(s) and source publication are appropriately acknowledged. If so indicated, certain images may not be included under the Creative Commons license. In such cases users will need to obtain permission from the license holder to reproduce the material. More details and guidelines concerning content reuse and adaptation can be found at http://www.intechopen.com/copyright-policy.html.

Notice

Statements and opinions expressed in the chapters are these of the individual contributors and not necessarily those of the editors or publisher. No responsibility is accepted for the accuracy of information contained in the published chapters. The publisher assumes no responsibility for any damage or injury to persons or property arising out of the use of any materials, instructions, methods or ideas contained in the book.

First published in London, United Kingdom, 2019 by IntechOpen
IntechOpen is the global imprint of INTECHOPEN LIMITED, registered in England and Wales, registration number: 11086078, The Shard, 25th floor, 32 London Bridge Street
London, SE19SG – United Kingdom
Printed in Croatia

British Library Cataloguing-in-Publication Data
A catalogue record for this book is available from the British Library

Additional hard and PDF copies can be obtained from orders@intechopen.com

Advances in Human and Machine Navigation Systems, Edited by Rastislav Róka
p. cm.
Print ISBN 978-1-83880-564-7
Online ISBN 978-1-83880-565-4
eBook (PDF) ISBN 978-1-83880-778-8

We are IntechOpen,
the world's leading publisher of
Open Access books
Built by scientists, for scientists

4,200+
Open access books available

116,000+
International authors and editors

125M+
Downloads

Our authors are among the

151
Countries delivered to

Top 1%
most cited scientists

12.2%
Contributors from top 500 universities

CLARIVATE ANALYTICS
BOOK
CITATION
INDEX
INDEXED

WEB OF SCIENCE™

Selection of our books indexed in the Book Citation Index
in Web of Science™ Core Collection (BKCI)

Interested in publishing with us?
Contact book.department@intechopen.com

Numbers displayed above are based on latest data collected.
For more information visit www.intechopen.com

Meet the editor

Rastislav Róka was born in Šaľa, Slovakia, on January 27, 1972. He received his MSc and PhD degrees in Telecommunications from the Slovak University of Technology, Bratislava, in 1995 and 2002. Since 1997, he has been working as a senior lecturer at the Institute of Multimedia Information and Communication Technologies, Faculty of Electrical Engineering and Information Technology, Slovak University of Technology, in Bratislava. Since 2009, he has been working as an associate professor at this institute. His teaching and educational activities are realized in areas of fixed transmission media, designing and planning of telecommunication networks, and optocommunication transmission systems. At present, his research activity is focused on signal transmission through optical transport, metropolitan, and access networks using advanced optical signal processing, including various multiplexing, modulation, and encoding techniques. His main effort is dedicated to effective utilization of optical fiber's transmission capacity in broadband optical networks by means of dynamic bandwidth and wavelength allocation algorithms applied in various advanced hybrid passive optical network infrastructures.

Contents

Preface IX

Section 1   **Introduction**   **1**

Chapter 1   **Introductory Chapter: Life Improving Advances in Navigation Systems** **3**
Rastislav Róka

Section 2   **Human Navigation Systems**   **7**

Chapter 2   **Walking Support System with Users' Circumstances** **9**
Kana Naitou and Kayoko Yamamoto

Chapter 3   **Vision-Based Tactile Paving Detection Method in Navigation Systems for Visually Impaired Persons** **29**
Anuar Bin Mohamed Kassim, Takashi Yasuno, Hiroshi Suzuki, Mohd Shahrieel Mohd Aras, Ahmad Zaki Shukor, Hazriq Izzuan Jaafar and Fairul Azni Jafar

Section 3   **Machine Navigation Systems**   **47**

Chapter 4   **Micro-Inertial-Aided High-Precision Positioning Method for Small-Diameter PIG Navigation** **49**
Lianwu Guan, Xu Xu, Yanbin Gao, Fanming Liu, Hanxiao Rong, Meng Wang and Aboelmagd Noureldin

Chapter 5   **Optimization of NOE Flights Sensors and Their Integration** **71**
Tamilselvam Nallusamy and Prasanalakshmi Balaji

Preface

Advances in Human and Machine Navigation Systems provides a platform for practicing researchers, academics, PhD students, and other scientists to design, analyze, evaluate, process, and implement diversiform issues of navigation systems, including life-improving advances in human navigation systems and advances improving machine navigation systems. The five chapters of the book demonstrate the capabilities of navigation systems to solve scientific and engineering problems with varying degrees of complexity.

The first chapter introduces the theme of life improving advances in navigation systems.The following two chapters are oriented towards advances in modern technologies improving various real-life aspects of populations. A walking support system that takes into account each user's health conditions, needs, and preferences is a real possibility for utilizing navigation systems by common users. Development of appropriate navigation systems for visually impaired persons who rely on guide canes to avoid obstructions or hazardous situations is also very important.

The last two chapters are dedicated to improving the functionalities of machine navigation systems. Utilizing navigation systems specialized for the pipeline industry can lead to life-improving advances. From the viewpoint of surrounding environments and public safety, it is important to eliminate negative influences of potential pipeline leakages. With advanced technological improvements and modern equipment, aircraft disasters are still happening. An enhancement strategy for nap-of-the-earth operations presents an optimization method using sensors. The establishment of new systems and improvement of existing ones may lead to the prevention of accidents while conducting nap-of-the-earth operations or flying at low levels.

I hope that beginners and professionals in the field will benefit from the details given in the chapters of this book.

Rastislav Róka
Slovak University of Technology
Institute of MICT
FEI STU Bratislava, Slovakia

Introduction

Chapter 1

Introductory Chapter: Life Improving Advances in Navigation Systems

Rastislav Róka

Additional information is available at the end of the chapter

http://dx.doi.org/10.5772/intechopen.82112

1. Introduction

Navigation systems are a study field that focuses on the process of monitoring and controlling the movement of an entity from one place to another. General, navigation systems may be entirely on board an entity, or they may be located elsewhere and communicate via radio or other signals with an entity, or they may use a combination of these methods. It means that navigation systems can refer to any skill that involves the determination of position and direction compared to known locations or patterns and, simultaneously, navigation strategies can include several general categories varying in the environment and navigator's substance. The book "Navigation Systems" provides a platform for researchers, academics, PhD students and other scientists to review, plan, design, analyze, evaluate, intend, process and implement diversiform issues of navigation systems. Topics of this book include some new methods, approaches and algorithms for applications in human and machine navigation systems. Five book chapters demonstrate capabilities and potentialities of navigation systems to solve scientific and engineering problems with a varied degree of the complexity. The first two chapters related to satellite navigation systems provide details of high-precision dynamic location and airborne double-antenna orientation approach. The second three chapters associated with human navigation systems demonstrate possibilities of utilizing modern technologies in navigation systems with the aim of helping common users and physically and/or visually impaired persons.

2. Advances improving satellite navigation systems

In the first part of the book, chapters are dedicated to improving functionalities of satellite navigation systems. A focus on characteristics of GPS and Beidou satellite navigation systems

IntechOpen

© 2018 The Author(s). Licensee IntechOpen. This chapter is distributed under the terms of the Creative Commons Attribution License (http://creativecommons.org/licenses/by/3.0), which permits unrestricted use, distribution, and reproduction in any medium, provided the original work is properly cited. [cc] BY

is interesting, especially when time and coordinate systems are utilized. For improving a receiver's accuracy, a high-precision dynamic localization can be considered in conjunction with an improved dual-mode positioning algorithm of the star selection and an optimal location algorithm. In order to solve a localization problem, an interesting solution can be applied to an approximate linearization system. For possible single-mode and dual-mode systems, requested equations for the filter should be prepared. It must be expected that a satellite navigation system composition is under composition and an improved algorithm is simulated and verified by the software. A positioning method of the dual-mode location and star selection can not only guarantee a positioning accuracy, but it should also improve system efficiency. Then, a design of the dual-mode navigation and positioning system can be advantageous.

When GPS and BeiDou satellite navigation systems are used for determining a course angle of the aircraft, then a focus on antenna orientation methods is interesting. The idea that global satellite navigation systems can not only provide the information in terms of location and time, but also the course angle of its carrier through processing of multiple antennas and specific data, can be considered. It is useful to utilize its advantages of none accumulative errors and its high orientation accuracy. For this reason, an observation model of satellite navigation systems can be established for proposing orientation methods. It must be emphases that any suggested resolution method of the carrier phase must be analyzed through a depth study. Also in this case, combined orientation and directional algorithms should have been verified in preference by the simulation program and hardware platform experiments.

3. Life improving advances in human navigation systems

In the first part of the book, chapters are oriented on advances in modern technologies improving various real life's aspect of populations. A walking support system that takes into account each user's health conditions, needs and preferences is a real possibility for utilizing of navigation systems by common users. The eventual system can be developed by integrating different partial systems into a single system. From a viewpoint of active users, it is very important to establish and conduct an interactive feedback. Based on the web questionnaire survey, the system usefulness can be increased for selecting a walking course. It is evident that the system should be used by different types of information terminals approximately in the same way. And, a system operation must be evaluated according to the purpose of effectively supporting users' walking activities. I hope that a functional and confirmed walking support system will be successfully widespread also in many cities and/or countries.

A development of appropriate navigation systems for visually impaired persons that are relying on guide canes in order to walk outside for avoiding any obstructions or hazardous situations is very important. Therefore, a tactile pavement detection system used the image recognition can be considered to advantage. Of course, some experiments must be conducted for detecting the tactile pavement and for identifying the shape of tactile patterns. For better proposal, the software environment including a special platform as guidance tools can be utilized. For notifying visually impaired persons, accurate auditory outputs must be included.

A development of the tactile pavement detection system can be prospective for easily detected and navigated purposes of serving for visually impaired persons.

Also utilizing of navigation systems specialized for a pipeline industry can lead for life improving. From a viewpoint of surrounding environments and a safety of civilian's lives, it is important to eliminate negative influences of potential pipeline leakages. And from these reasons, an attention should be focused on a pipeline inspection gauge that could accomplish a variety of pipeline defects. Because inspections should be executed effectively, then these defects must be localized precisely by installing various detecting and positioning sensors. So, a proposal of relevant navigation systems can be prepared application mechanisms with advanced position methods researched for improving the overall positioning precision. With regard to demands, proposed methods and research conclusions are expected to be verified by simulation experiments using the indoor wheel robot platform and appropriate experiments.

I hope that beginners and professionals in the field would benefit by going through details given in these chapters of the book.

Author details

Rastislav Róka

Address all correspondence to: rastislav.roka@stuba.sk

Slovak University of Technology, Bratislava, Slovakia

Human Navigation Systems

Chapter 2

Walking Support System with Users' Circumstances

Kana Naitou and Kayoko Yamamoto

Additional information is available at the end of the chapter

http://dx.doi.org/10.5772/intechopen.78345

Abstract

In Japan, the central government started the promotion of citizens' health by self-supervision in 2000, and walking is recently recognized as the most popular sport for many generations. Based on this background, the present study aimed to design, develop, operate, and evaluate a walking support system, which takes into account the users' circumstances (each user's health conditions, needs, and preferences). The system was developed by integrating Web-GIS (geographic information systems) as a base system and social networking services (SNS) as well as a registration system of walking information into a single system. Additionally, the system was operated for 5 weeks in Chofu City in Tokyo Metropolis, Japan, and the total number of users was 73. Based on the results of the Web questionnaire survey, the usefulness of the system when selecting a walking course was high, and the further use of each function can be expected by the continuous operation of the system. From the results of access analysis of users' log data, it is evident that the system has been used by two types of information terminals approximately in the same way, and that the entire system has been used according to the purpose of the present study, which is to effectively support the users' walking.

Keywords: walking, walkability, users' circumstances, Web-GIS, SNS, registration system of walking information

1. Introduction

In Japan, the central government declared "Healthy Japan 21" in 2000, put the Health Promotion Law into force in 2003, and spelled out the measures and policies for the promotion of citizens' health by self-supervision. It is pointed out that the increase of human body activities centering on walking should lead to suppress cardiovascular diseases and cancer and prolong human lifespan. Therefore, the main objective of the "Healthy Japan 21 first

IntechOpen

© 2018 The Author(s). Licensee IntechOpen. This chapter is distributed under the terms of the Creative Commons Attribution License (http://creativecommons.org/licenses/by/3.0), which permits unrestricted use, distribution, and reproduction in any medium, provided the original work is properly cited. (cc) BY

(2000–2012)" was to increase the numbers of walking steps and those who continue some physical exercises (Ministry of Health, Labour, and Welfare [1]). In the "Healthy Japan 21 second (2013–2023)," the improvement of the environment to continue walking was added to the main objective (Ministry of Health, Labor, and Welfare [2]). Additionally, according to the public opinion survey conducted by the Ministry of Education, Culture, Sports, Science and Technology [3], it was evident that walking is the most popular sport among Japanese because it is easy for everyone to start it. In this way, regardless of age or sex, it is possible for everyone to easily work on walking in everyday life. Walking is the most suitable physical activity (PA) especially for elder people because it is possible for them to prevent the drop of physical strength and body ability by aging.

On the other hand, currently, Japan finds itself in the position of a "developed" country, facing many serious challenges to declining birth rate, aging population, and the environment and energy issues, that it must address head-on, challenges, which other countries will 1 day also be facing. Therefore, in most of the Japanese cities, it is essential to realize "compact town development" that puts homes and places of work in close proximity to each other appears to be one effective way of making it easier to face the above serious challenges. Walkability is a concept to comprehensively show the situations of the physical environment of the urban space to support and promote walking in everyday life. An environmental approach, which ameliorates the urban space to improve and promote residents' health, attracts attention all over the world, and walkability is placed as the important point. An increase in the number of steps, that is, an increase in walking time, is related to the walkability factors such as sidewalks, landscapes, and traffic safety, which influence on walking time (Inoue et al. [4]).

One of the methods to explicitly provide geospatial information related to the above walkability factors is geographic information systems (GIS). GIS is a powerful tool to overlay, analyze, maintain, and share various kinds of geospatial information on the digital map, referring to the longitude, latitude, and height. Therefore, it is possible to visually display geospatial information concerning the above walkability factors on the digital map of the Web-GIS to efficiently support walking.

Based on the background mentioned above, the present study aims to design, develop, operate, and evaluate a walking support system, which integrates a Web-GIS as a base system, an social networking services (SNS), and a registration system of walking information, while taking into account the users' needs, which can change according to the circumstances (each user's health conditions, needs, and preferences). The system efficiently provides various information related to walking to support many generations, and it is expected that it will enable users to control their health by themselves.

2. Related work

The system in the present study was developed by integrating plural systems such as Web-GIS, SNS as well as the registration system of walking information into a single system. Therefore, the present study is related to three study fields, namely, (A) studies regarding walkability, (B) studies regarding activity support system developed by GIS, and (C) studies regarding social media GIS.

In A studies regarding walkability, as this topic attracts attention just in recent years, there were few preceding studies until now. Cerin et al. [5] examined the factorial and criterion validity of the neighborhood environment walkability scale (NEWS) and developed an abbreviated version (NEWS-A). Kondo et al. [6] investigated the actual association between physical activity (PA) and neighborhood environments (NE) focused on either objectively measuring the NE or the residents' perception of NE in Japan. Inoue et al. [7] conducted a questionnaire survey to investigate the relationship between living environment and walking, just targeting Japanese.

In B studies regarding activity support system developed by GIS, Ishizuka et al. [8] proposed a similarity search method for the movement tracking data of tourists obtained from their location data and its text information. Kurata [9] developed an automatic generation system for sightseeing courses using Web-GIS and genetic algorithm (GA). Kawamura [10] proposed the use of standard tags related to sightseeing on SNS and set up a Website to organize tourism information of Hokkaido on the Internet. Sasaki et al. [11] gathered information concerning local resources and developed a system that supports the sightseeing activities of each user. Fujitsuka et al. [12] used the pattern mining method, which lists and extracts the time series action when touring sightseeing spots, and developed an outing plan recommendation system. Ueda et al. [13] generated post-activity information from the sightseeing activities of the users and developed a tourism support system, which shares such information as prior information for other users. Okuzono et al. [14] took into consideration the preferences of several people using photos, and proposed a system that recommends sightseeing spots.

Fujita et al. [15] developed a navigation system using augmented reality (AR), Web-GIS, and social media, in order to support sightseeing activities during normal occasions and evacuation in case of a disaster. Zhou et al. [16] develop a sightseeing spot recommendation system using AR, Web-GIS, and SNS. Based on these results, Mizutani et al. [17] developed a sightseeing spot recommendation system taking into account the change in circumstances of users. Abe et al. [18] developed a tourism information system with language-barrier-free interfaces, mainly targeting foreign visitors. Mizushima et al. [19] proposed a service data model in design support system for sightseeing tours, based on tourists' three types of requests (geographical, time, and meaning information). Yamamoto [20] developed sightseeing navigation system, using 2D and 3D digital maps of the Web-GIS, and just targeting foreign visitors.

In C studies regarding social media GIS, Yanagisawa et al. [21] as well as Nakahara et al. [22] developed an information sharing GIS, using Web-GIS, SNS, and Wiki, with the purpose of storing and sharing information of the local community. Yamada et al. [23] and Okuma et al. [24] developed a social media GIS, which strengthened the social media function of the information sharing GIS mentioned above. Based on such systems developed from preceding studies, Murakoshi et al. [25] and Yamamoto et al. [26] developed a social media GIS supporting the continuous use of disaster information during normal occasions and in case of a disaster. In addition, based on these social media GIS, Ikeda et al. [27] developed a social recommendation GIS to accumulate sightseeing spot information and recommend sightseeing spot according to the preference of each user.

Among the preceding studies in related fields as listed above, B and C support the tour planning and accumulating and sharing of spot information for activity support. Additionally, the existing system developed in B and C is not suitable to support walking. Against the above-mentioned preceding studies, the present study demonstrates the originality to develop a walking support system, by integrating Web-GIS as a base system, an SNS, and a registration system of walking information, and targeting many generations. Furthermore, referring to Inoue et al. [7] in A, the present study shows the usefulness to provide important geospatial information from the viewpoint of walkability to users, and support them to select their suitable walking courses in response to their preferences, aptitudes, and situations.

3. System design

3.1. System configuration

The system of the present study is developed by means of Web-GIS, an SNS, and a registration system of walking information, as shown in **Figure 1**. The system enables to visualize the information related to outlines, height, and sightseeing spot on the digital maps of the Web-GIS. Therefore, it is possible for users to efficiently obtain the necessary information related to walking. Since the system is connected with external SNS (Twitter), it is possible for users to share various information related to walking, and displaying the tweets with a specific hashtag submitted by others. Additionally, it is also possible for users to register their walking information such as the number and time of their steps. Users can freely confirm their registered information, which is maintained in the database of the system.

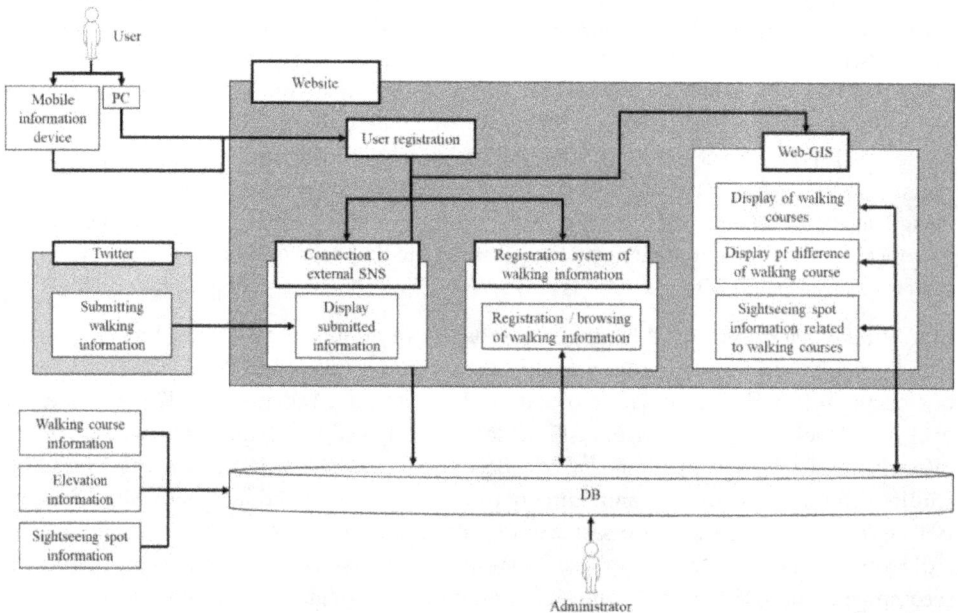

Figure 1. System design.

The usability of the system mentioned in the previous section can be summarized in the following three points, by means of the design described in detail as shown in **Figure 1**.

1. Reduction of the burden of information obtainment: Users can select their walking course, considering various information such as distance, height, and sightseeing spot. In general, it takes a long-time to gather such an information provided in multifarious formats. However, in the system, since the geospatial information related every walking course is displayed on the digital maps of the Web-GIS, users can reduce the time to obtain their necessary information, and receive the support of their selections.

2. Visual confirmation of geospatial information: It is difficult to grasp the geospatial information related to walking courses and sightseeing spots at a glance, just referring to guidebooks, and pamphlets. Since the above geospatial information is displayed using Web-GIS, the user can visually confirm it on the digital map at first glance.

3. Effective support for users' activities: Though it is possible to take the record of the number of walking steps using a pedometer, it is not easy to confirm the information related to walking courses, and comments. However, the system enables users to manually register their numbers and time of their steps, and their comments on the selected walking courses. Confirming these to grasp the present situation of walking at fixed interval, it is expected that users should control their health on their own initiative.

3.2. Target information terminals

Though the system is meant to be used from PCs or mobile devices, as there is no difference in functions on different information terminals, the same function can be used from any device. PCs are assumed to be used indoors for gathering and register walking information. On the other hand, mobile devices are assumed to be used both indoors and outdoors to gather information concerning sightseeing spots.

3.3. System operation environment

The system operates using the Web server, database server, and the GIS server. **Figure 2** shows the operating environment of the system. The Web server and database server both use the Heroku, which is a Platform as a Service (PaaS) provided by the Salesforce company. For the GIS server, the ArcGIS Online was used. The Web application developed with the system was implemented using PHP and JavaScript.

3.4. Design of each server

3.4.1. Web-GIS

As there are a variety of Web-GIS types, it is necessary to select the most suitable type according to the purpose of using the system. In terms of convenience, the system should be used without having to download any special software, which would be inconvenient for users, and it would be desirable if it could be used by accessing the Website on any PC or mobile device connected to the Internet. Therefore, a series of the GIS provided by Environmental Systems Research Institute, Inc. (ESRI) was selected to develop the Web-GIS in the present study. The detailed design of the Web-GIS is as follows:

1. Display of walking courses on the digital maps

   At first, the layers were created by plotting the geospatial information related to walking courses and sightseeing spots on the basic digital maps, and these were overlaid to create the Web maps, using the ArcGIS Online provided by ESRI. These Web maps were disclosed on the Website as the Web-GIS, using the ArcGIS application programming interface (API) for JavaScript provided by ESRI.

2. Display of elevation difference of walking course on the digital maps

   The elevation difference is related to exercise strength and influences on the selection of walking courses. Therefore, using the above Web maps and a Web application template included in the GitHub provided by ESRI, elevation difference of walking course was displayed on the digital maps, and was also disclosed on the Website as the Web-GIS, using the ArcGIS API for JavaScript.

3. Display of sightseeing spot information related to walking courses on the digital maps

   Inoue et al. [4] pointed out landscape is one of the most important walkability factors. Therefore, the system provides the sightseeing spot information related to walking courses to the users. For that, the detailed information and images related to walking courses in the operation target area in the present study were gathered, and they were displayed on the Web maps using the Web application template included in the GitHub. These Web maps were also disclosed on the Website as the Web-GIS, using the ArcGIS API for JavaScript.

3.4.2. Connection to external SNS

The system is connected to Twitter, and users can submit and search for the information related to walking courses and sightseeing spots. The system enables to obtain the tweets with a specific hashtag, and display them on the homepage.

3.4.3. Registration system of walking information

Users can register and confirm the date, selected walking course, number and time of steps, walkability, and comments on their personal pages. These are accumulated in the PostgreSQL connected with the Heroku application. The Web application developed with the system was implemented using PHP and JavaScript. Therefore, it is expected that users should reasonably continue walking and control their health by themselves.

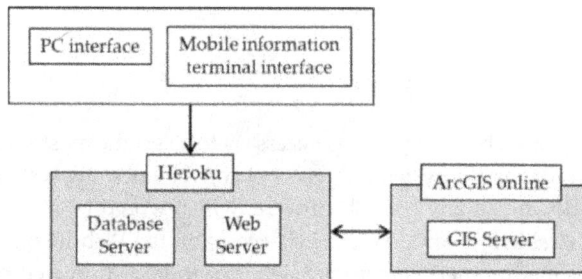

Figure 2. System operating environment.

4. System development

The system will implement unique functions for users, which will be mentioned below, in response to the aim of the present study, as mention in Section 1. In order to implement these several unique functions, the system was developed by integrating plural systems into a single system, and is also connected with external SNS.

4.1. The frontend of the system

4.1.1. Login function

Users register when using the system for the first time. After moving from the login page to the registration page, users can register and submit the "ID," "password," "name," "age," "gender," and "email address." Next, after logging in to the system on the login page, users can move to the homepage.

4.1.2. Display function of walking course

After selecting a favorite course in the menu bar on the homepage, users can go the page for the display function of walking course (**Figure 3**) to confirm its outline on the digital map of the Web-GIS. The selected walking course is clearly displayed as a line on the digital map.

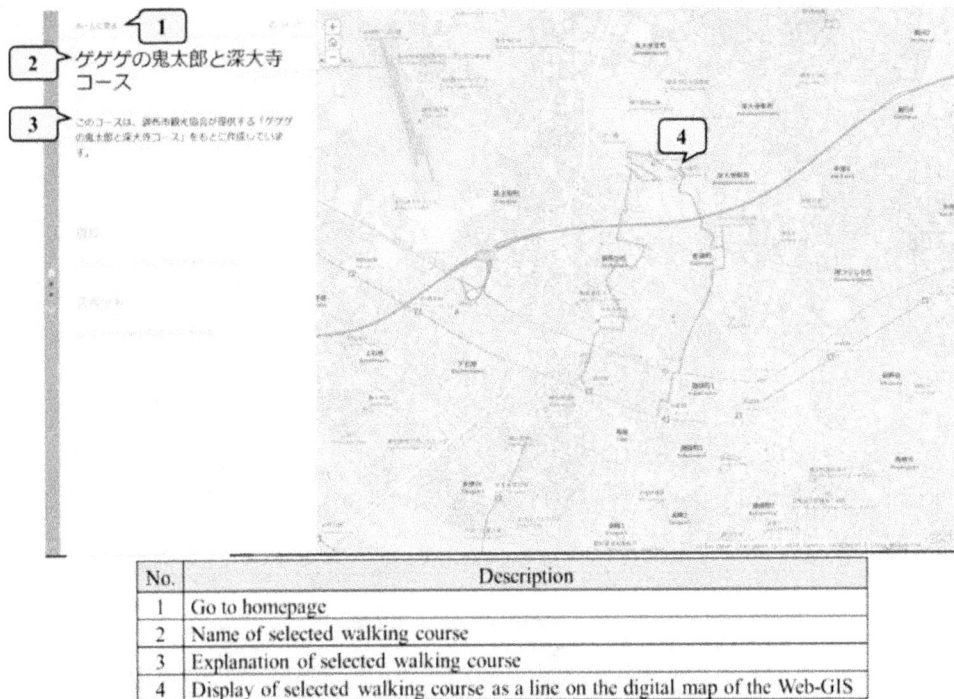

No.	Description
1	Go to homepage
2	Name of selected walking course
3	Explanation of selected walking course
4	Display of selected walking course as a line on the digital map of the Web-GIS

Figure 3. Page for the display function of walking course.

4.1.3. Display function of the elevation difference of walking course

After confirming the outline of the selected walking course, by clicking its line on the digital map, users can go to the page for the display function of the elevation difference of walking course (**Figure 4**) to confirm the elevation difference. In the graph shown in **Figure 4**, the vertical axis indicates elevation (m), and the horizontal axis indicates the distance (km). By moving the cursor in the graph, the location corresponding to the walking course is displayed by a blue circle.

4.1.4. Viewing function of the sightseeing spot information related to walking courses

After confirming the elevation difference of walking course, by scrolling the menu bar on the left side of the screen downward, users can go to the page for the viewing function of sightseeing spot information related to walking courses (**Figure 5**) to view the sightseeing spot information around walking courses (location, explanation, and image).

4.1.5. Viewing function of the information submitted by twitter

After login to the system, on the left side of the home page, users can view the information related walking courses, and sightseeing spots submitted by Twitter. The information is updated in real time, and users can view others' tweets.

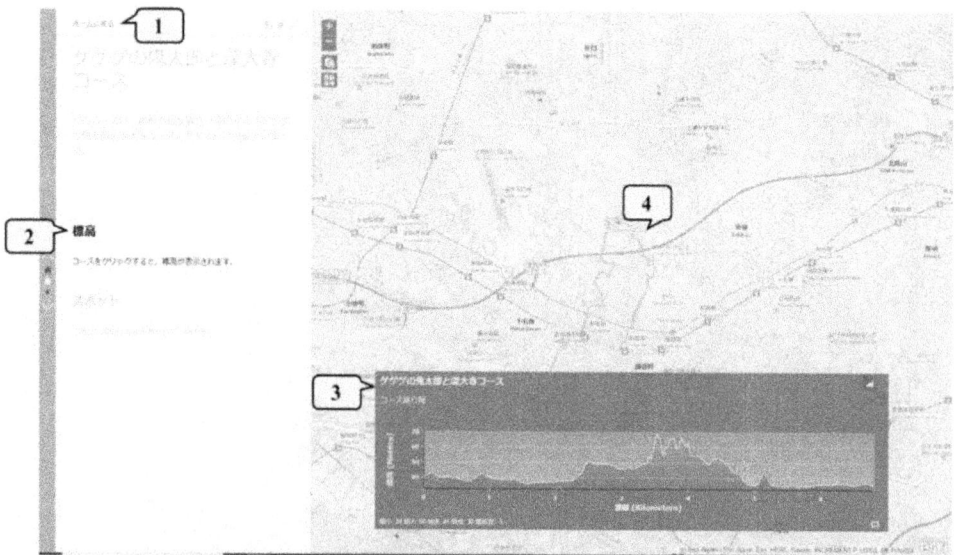

No.	Description
1	Go to homepage
2	Elevation difference of the selected walking course
3	Elevation difference of selected walking course displayed by a graph
4	Display of selected walking course as a line on the digital map of the Web-GIS

Figure 4. Page for the display function of the elevation difference of walking course.

No.	Description
1	Go to homepage
2	Sightseeing spot information related to selected walking course
3	Images of sightseeing spot information related to selected walking course
4	Image and explanation of sightseeing spot information related to selected walking course

Figure 5. Page for the viewing function of the sightseeing spot information related to walking courses.

4.1.6. Registration function of walking information

After logging in to the system, by selecting "Registration of walking information" in the menu bar on the left side of the homepage, users can go to the page for the registration function of walking information (**Figure 6**) to register, and confirm the information related to their walking history.

4.2. The backend of the system

4.2.1. Process concerning the member registration and login

All of users' registered information is accumulated in the PostgreSQL connected with the Heroku application. Each user's password is, respectively, made a hash using the Hash function of PHP, and it is accumulated in the database. All of users' registered information and registration time are also accumulated in the database. At the time of login, each user's password is made a hash, and login process is conducted, if a password accords with an ID in the database.

4.2.2. Process concerning the connection with SNS

The tweets related to walking courses and sightseeing spots are obtained using the Twitter OAuth library. Specifically, the tweets with the hashtag "#chfgis" can be accumulated as new information in the system, and these are updated in real time.

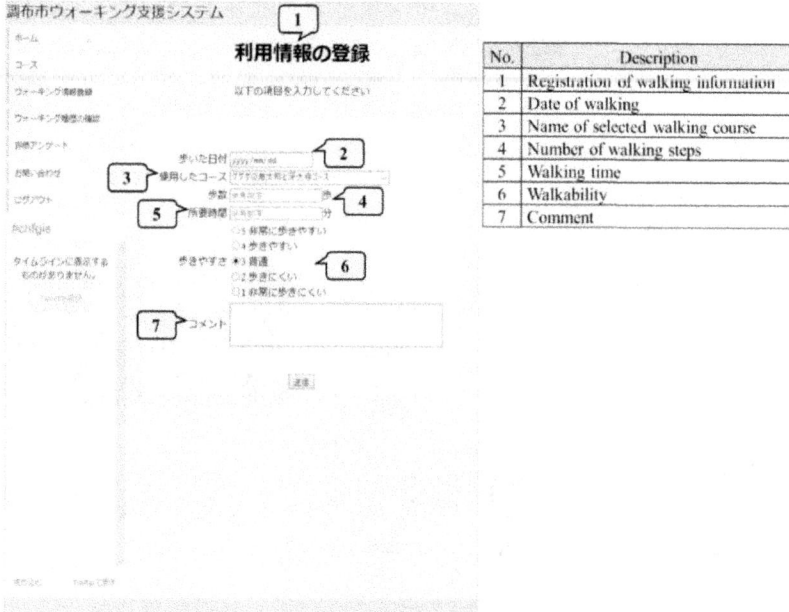

Figure 6. Page for the registration function of walking information.

No.	Description
1	Registration of walking information
2	Date of walking
3	Name of selected walking course
4	Number of walking steps
5	Walking time
6	Walkability
7	Comment

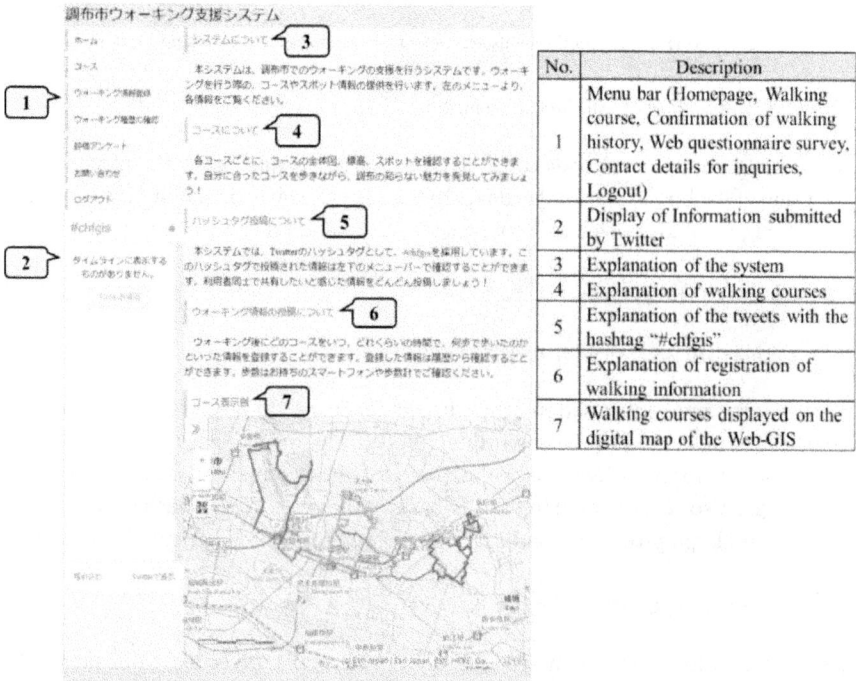

Figure 7. User's PC screen and mobile device screen.

No.	Description
1	Menu bar (Homepage, Walking course, Confirmation of walking history, Web questionnaire survey, Contact details for inquiries, Logout)
2	Display of Information submitted by Twitter
3	Explanation of the system
4	Explanation of walking courses
5	Explanation of the tweets with the hashtag "#chfgis"
6	Explanation of registration of walking information
7	Walking courses displayed on the digital map of the Web-GIS

4.2.3. Process concerning registration of walking information

All of the users' registered information as well as ID and personal information is maintained in the PostgreSQL database server. Users can view and revise such information displayed on the users' personal pages.

4.3. System interface

The system has two types of interfaces: The PC screen and mobile device screen for users (**Figure 7**), and the PC screen for the administrator. In the latter, the "ID," "password," "name," "age," "gender," and "email address" of all users can be checked on a list. Additionally, due to the simplification of user management using graphic user interface (GUI), procedures such as the deletion of unauthorized users can be done without depending on the IT literacy of the administrator.

5. Operation

5.1. Operation overview

Regarding the operation target area, the Chofu City in Tokyo Metropolis, Japan, was selected. One reason for this selection is that it has popular walking courses and sightseeing spots in the city. The second is that the city consists of flat terrain and gentle slopes, and such a topography condition is suitable for walking.

The system was operated over a period of 5 weeks (from 12/15/2017 to 1/22/2018) with those inside and outside the operation target area. Whether inside or outside the operation target area, the operation of the system was advertised using the Website of the authors' lab as well as Twitter and Facebook.

5.2. Operation result

Users of the system are shown in **Table 1**. The system has a total of 73 users with 48 male and 25 female users. Regarding age groups, there are many male and female users in their 20s making up 56% of the total. Subsequently, those in their 50s were 15%; those in their 40s were 11%; those in their 30s were 7%; those in their 10s were 6%; and those in their 60s, and above were 6%. The number of people who used the registration function of walking information was only 5, about 7% of the total number of users, and the number of walking information registered was 21. However, by using the system over a long period, it is expected that further registration of walking information.

5.3. Management of submitted information by administrators during the operation

Every user's submissions of information and image files are all accumulated as data in the database of the system. Administrators manage users and check submitted information using a list screen designed especially for the purpose. Administrators can take the measure of suspending accounts of users who have made inappropriate transmissions or behaved

Age groups of users	10–19	20–29	30–39	40–49	50–59	60–69	70-	Total
Number of users	4	40	5	9	11	2	2	73
Number of Web questionnaire survey respondents	4	23	1	4	3	1	0	36
Valid response rate (%)	100.0	57.5	20.0	44.4	27.3	50.0	0.0	49.3

Table 1. Breakdown of system users and Web questionnaire survey respondents.

inappropriately, and if by any chance an inappropriate submission is made, administrators can delete the submission with just one click. Due to these features, there is no need for administrators to search to see whether or not inappropriate submissions of information have been made within the system; therefore, their burden can be lessened.

6. Evaluation

After the end of the operation, a Web questionnaire survey and access analysis of users' log data were conducted in order to evaluate the system developed in the present study.

6.1. Evaluation based on Web questionnaire survey

6.1.1. Overview of the Web questionnaire survey

Along with the purpose of the present study, a Web questionnaire survey was implemented in order to conduct an evaluation on the use of the system, an evaluation on system function, and an evaluation of the entire system. The Web questionnaire survey was conducted for 1 week after the start of the operation. **Table 1** also shows an overview of the Web questionnaire survey. As shown in **Table 1**, 36 out of 73 users submitted their Web questionnaire survey, and the valid response rate was 49.3%.

6.1.2. Evaluation on the use of the system

Regarding the viewing frequency of the Website, 75% viewed the Website every day, and 19% viewed the Website several times a week. Regarding the access methods to the system, 44% were PCs, and 56% were mobile information terminals. Therefore, it was made evident that the system developed using the Web-GIS as a base system is useful. Additionally, because the access method from the PC and the mobile information terminal was hardly different, it was effective to make the system available from both terminals.

6.1.3. Evaluation of system function

The evaluation results for the usefulness of the main functions to support walking are shown in **Figure 8**. Specifically, **Figure 8** shows the results that asked the users whether these items are useful.

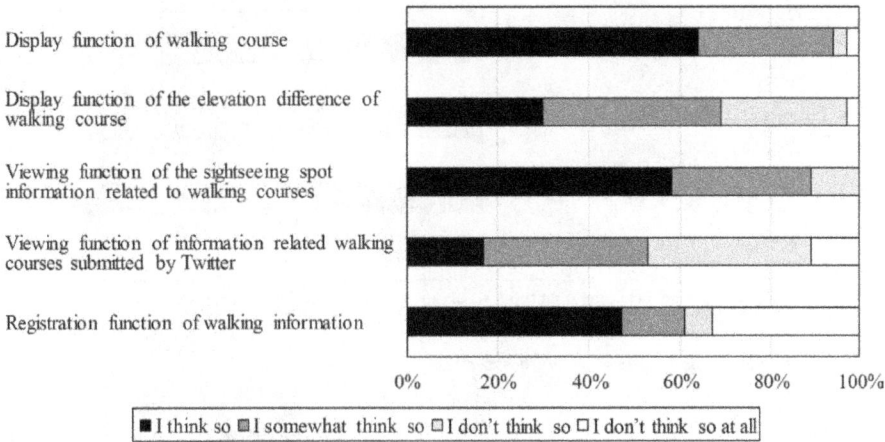

Figure 8. Evaluation of the usefulness of the main functions to support walking.

Regarding the display function of walking course, 94% answered "I think so" or "I somewhat think so," 3% answered "I don't think so," and 3% answered "I don't think so at all". Because it is important to select a suitable walking course, the usefulness of this function was highly evaluated. Regarding the display function of the elevation difference of walking course, 69% answered "I think so" or "I somewhat think so," 28% answered "I do not think so," and 3% answered "I do not think so at all". The reason for this result is that 56% of the users of the system were in their 20s, and they did not pay attention to the elevation difference of walking courses.

Regarding the viewing function of the sightseeing spot information related to walking courses, 89% answered "I think so" or "I somewhat think so," and 11% answered "I don't think so." Because most respondents tended to select the walking courses with a lot of sightseeing spots. Regarding the viewing function of information related walking courses submitted by Twitter, 53% answered "I think so" or "I somewhat think so," 36% answered "I don't think so," and 11% answered "I don't think so at all." Consequently, 47% of the users did not highly evaluate the usefulness of this function. Because these users did not have their Twitter accounts, and it was impossible for them to directly submit information to the system.

Regarding the registration function of walking information, 61% answered "I think so" or "I somewhat think so," 6% answered "I don't think so," and 33% answered "I don't think so at all." However, the function may be used more often by the continuous operation of the system, and this may advance the usefulness of the system when walking.

6.1.4. Evaluation of the entire system

The evaluation results for the usefulness of the entire system are shown in **Figure 9**. As with **Figures 8** and **9** shows the results that asked the users whether these items are useful.

Regarding the entire system when walking, 81% answered "I think so" or "I somewhat think so," and it was evident that the system was highly evaluated. Though it is necessary

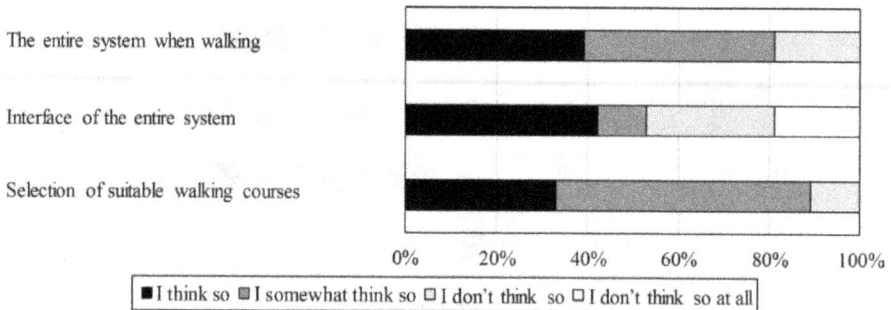

Figure 9. Evaluation on the usefulness of the entire system.

to improve some functions according to the users' evaluation results, it can be said that the system was useful to select a favorite walking course in responding to each user's preferences, aptitudes, and situations.

Regarding the interface of the entire system, though 53% answered "I think so" or "I somewhat think so," 47% answered "I don't think so" or "I don't think so at all." The reason for this result is that the interface optimized for mobile information terminals was not developed. Regarding the selection of suitable walking courses, 89% answered "I think so" or "I somewhat think so." Therefore, the system is useful for almost users to select their suitable walking course.

6.2. Evaluation based on results of access analysis

In the present study, an access analysis was conducted using the users' log data during the operation period. This analysis was conducted using Google Analytics, which is a Web access analysis service provided by Google. A PHP program with the analysis code made using Google Analytics was created, and for the target Websites for the access analysis, the access log was obtained by scanning the PHP program made for the access analysis of the program in each page within that Website.

The access method to the system is shown in **Table 2**. There is hardly any difference in the use of PCs and mobile devices as an access method. This is because smartphones are now often used as an easy way to obtain information. Therefore, the system design, which was made to eliminate the differences in obtainable information depending on the type of device and to make the system available to all types of devices, can be considered effective.

The number of views of each walking course is shown in **Table 3**. As it is made clear in **Table 3**, the most popular walking courses were "Course of Gegege no Kitaro (a Japanese famous cartoon setting in Chofu City) and Jindai-ji Temple." Subsequently, walking courses of "City of the Movie, Chofu, and Tama River," and "Art and culture in Sengawa District" were popular. Because these walking courses are displayed on the top of the menu, it was easy for users to select them. Additionally, there are a lot of well-known sightseeing spots around these walking courses, and users tended to select them. Among the four courses of city walking, the short ones are more popular than the long ones.

Access method	Number of sessions	Percentage (%)
PC	154	56.2
Smartphone	230	37.7
Tablet	25	6.1

Table 2. Access methods.

Name of walking course	Number of views
Course of Gegege no Kitaro (a Japanese cartoon setting in Chofu City) and Jindai-ji Temple	121
Course of City of the Movie, Chofu and Tama River	39
Course of art and culture in Sengawa District	34
Course of Kondo Isami and green space	18
Course of city walking 2013 (Jindai-ji Temple and Kaniyama)	23
Course of city walking 2013 (Fuda and Gojuku Districts)	12
Short course of city walking 2014	40
Long course of city walking 2014	9
Short course of city walking 2014	27
Long course of city walking 2014	14

Table 3. Number of views of walking course.

6.3. Identification of measures to improve the system

Based on the results of the evaluation of the operation in this section, measures for using the system even more effectively were summarized into the two points below.

1. Thought the system mainly provided the existing information related to walking courses and sightseeing spots, it did not provide real-time information related to users' present location, weather and traffic conditions. Therefore, it is necessary to examine the contents and providing method of information.

2. Though the information submitted by Twitter is accumulated in the system, it was impossible for the users who did not have their Twitter accounts to submit any information. Therefore, it is desirable to add a new function to directly submit information to the system.

7. Conclusion

In the present study, after designing and developing the system (Sections 3 and 4), the operation (Section 5) as well as the evaluation, and extraction of improvement measures (Section 6) were conducted. The present study can be summarized into the following three points.

1. In order to support many generations for walking, while taking into account the users' needs, which can change according to the circumstances, a system which integrated Web-GIS as a base system, SNS as well as the registration system of walking information was designed and developed. By doing so, the reduction of the burden of information obtainment, the visual confirmation of geospatial information, and the effective support for users' activities were made possible. Chofu City in Tokyo Metropolis, Japan was selected as the operation target area, and the system operation and evaluation were conducted.

2. The operation of the system was conducted over a period of 5 weeks targeting those inside and outside the operation target area, and a Web questionnaire survey was conducted toward all users. Based on the results of the Web questionnaire survey, the usefulness of the system when selecting a walking course was high, and the further use of each function can be expected by continuous operation.

3. From the results of access analysis of users' log data, it is evident that the system has been used by different types of devices just as it was designed for, and that the system has been used according to the purpose of the present study, which is to support the walking activities of users. Therefore, on the next step of the present study, it is necessary to inspect this point by the even more long-term operation of the system.

As future study projects, the improvement of the system based on the results in the previous section as well as the enhancement of the significance of using the system by gaining more results in other urban areas can be raised.

Acknowledgements

In the operation of the walking support system and the Web questionnaires survey of the present study, enormous cooperation was received from those mainly in Chofu City and the neighboring areas in Tokyo Metropolis, Japan. We would like to take this opportunity to gratefully acknowledge them.

Conflict of interest

The authors declare that there is no conflict of interest that could be perceived as prejudicing the impartiality of the research reported.

Author details

Kana Naitou* and Kayoko Yamamoto

*Address all correspondence to: n1830077@edu.cc.uec.ac.jp

University of Electro-Communications, Tokyo, Japan

References

[1] Ministry of Health, Labour and Welfare: Promotion of National Health Promotion Exercise (Health Japan 21) in the 21st Century; 2000. p. 209

[2] Ministry of Health, Labour and Welfare: Final Evaluation of National Health Promotion Exercise (Health Japan 21) in the 21st Century; 2013. p. 136

[3] Ministry of Education, Culture, Sports, Science and Technology: Public Opinion Survey on Physical Strength and Sports; 2013. p. 223

[4] Inoue S. Urban walkability and lifestyle diseases. Journal of livable city studies. 2011; **2**:39-50

[5] Cerin E, Saelens BE, Sallis JF, Frank LD. Neighborhood environment walkability scale: Validity and development of a short form. Medicine and Science in Sports and Exercise. 2006;**38**(9):1682-1691. DOI: 10.1249/01.mss.0000227639.83607.4d

[6] Kondo K, Lee JS, Kawakubo K, Kataoka Y, Asami Y, Mori K, Umezaki M, Yamauchi T, Takagi H, Sunagawa H, Akabayashi A. Association between daily physical activity and neighborhood environments. Environmental Health and Preventive Medicine. 2009;**14**(3):196-206. DOI: 10.1007/s12199-009-0081-1

[7] Inoue S, Ohya Y, Odagiri Y, Takamiya T, Ishii K, Kitabayashi M, Suijo K, Sallis JF, Shimomitsu T. Association between perceived neighborhood environment and walking among adults in 4 cities in Japan. Journal of Epidemiology. 2010;**20**(4):277-286. DOI: 10.2188/jea.JE20090120

[8] Ihizuka J, Suzuki Y, Kawagoe K. Method for searching for similarities in data on movement paths, designed to support sightseeing in Kyoto. The special interest group technical reports of information processing Society of Japan. CVIM, Computer Vision and Image Media. 2007;**2007**(1):17-23

[9] Kurata Y. Introducing a hot-start mechanism to a web-based tour planner ct-planner and increasing its coverage areas. In: Papers and Proceedings of the Geographic Information Systems Association of Japan; 2012. Vol. 21. p. 4

[10] Kawamura H. Efforts to spread standard tags in Hokkaido tourist information, and the development of Kyun-Channel. Journal of Digital Practice. 2012;**3**(4):272-280

[11] Sasaki J, Uetake T, Horikawa M, Sugawara M. Development of personal sightseeing support system during long-term stay. In: Proceedings of 75th National Convention of IPSJ; 2013. pp. 727-728

[12] Fujitsuka T, Harada T, Sato H, Takadama, K. Recommendation system for sightseeing plan using pattern mining to evaluate time series action. In: Proceedings of the Annual Conference on Society of Instrument and Control Engineering 2014; 2014;SS12-10. pp. 802-807

[13] Ueda T, Ooka R, Kumano K, Tarumi H, Hayashi T, Yaegashi, M. Sightseeing Support System to Support Generation/Sharing of Sightseeing Information, The Special Interest

Group Technical Reports of IPSJ: Information system and Social Environment (IS), 2015; **2015-IS-131**(4). pp. 1-7

[14] Okuzono M, Muta M, Hirano H, Masuko S, Hoshino, J. Recommendation System of Sightseeing Area for Groups, The Special Interest Group Technical Reports of IPSJ: Human Computer Interaction (HCI), 2015;**2015-HCI-162**(19):1-8

[15] Fujita S, Yamamoto K. Development of dynamic real-time navigation system. International Journal of Advanced Computer Science and Applications. 2016;**7**(11):116-130. DOI: 10.14569/IJACSA.2016.071116

[16] Zhou J, Yamamoto K. Development of the system to support tourists' excursion behavior using augmented reality. International Journal of Advanced Computer Science and Applications. 2016;**7**(7):197-209. DOI: 10.14569/IJACSA.2016.070727

[17] Mizutani Y, Yamamoto K. A sightseeing spot recommendation system that takes into account the change in circumstances of users. International Journal of Geo-Information. 2017;**6**(10):303. DOI: 10.3390/ijgi6100303

[18] Abe S, Miki D, Yamamoto K. A tourism information system with language-barrier-free interfaces for foreign visitors. In: Proceedings of the International Conference and Management (BEM) and International Conference on Marketing and Tourism; 2017. pp. 58-66

[19] Mizushima T, Hirota J, Oizumi K, Aoyama K. Service data model in design support system for sightseeing tours. In: Sawatani Y, Spohrer J, Kwan S, Takenaka T, editors. Serviceology for Smart Service System. Berlin and Heidelberg, Germany: Springer; 2017. pp. 55-64. DOI: 10.1007/978-4-431-56074-6_7

[20] Yamamoto K. Navigation system for foreign tourists in Japan. Journal Environmental Science and Engineering. 2018;**10B**(6):521-541. DOI: 10.17265/2162-5263/2017.10.004

[21] Yanagisawa T, Yamamoto K. Study on information sharing GIS to accumulate local knowledge in local communities. Theory and Applications of GIS. 2012;**20**(1):61-70

[22] Nakahara H, Yanagisawa T, Yamamoto K. Study on a Web-GIS to support the communication of regional knowledge in regional communities: Focusing on regional residents' experiential knowledge. Socio-Informatics. 2012;**1**(2):77-92

[23] Yamada S, Yamamoto K. Development of social media GIS for information exchange between regions. International Journal of Advanced Computer Science and Applications. 2013;**4**(8):62-73. DOI: 10.14569/IJACSA.2013.040810

[24] Okuma T, Yamamoto K. Study on a social media GIS to accumulate urban disaster information: Accumulation of disaster information during normal times for disaster reduction measures. Socio-Informatics. 2013;**2**(2):49-65

[25] Murakoshi T, Yamamoto K. Study on a social media GIS to support the utilization of disaster information: For disaster reduction measures from normal times to disaster outbreak times. Socio-Informatics. 2014;**3**(1):17-30

[26] Yamamoto K, Fujita S. Development of social media GIS to support information utilization from normal times to disaster outbreak times. International Journal of Advanced Computer Science and Applications. 2015;6(9):1-14. DOI: 10.14569/IJACSA.2015.060901

[27] Ikeda T, Yamamoto K. Development of social recommendation GIS for tourist spots. International Journal of Advanced Computer Science and Applications. 2014;5(12):8-21. DOI: 10.14569/IJACSA.2014.051202

Vision-Based Tactile Paving Detection Method in Navigation Systems for Visually Impaired Persons

Anuar Bin Mohamed Kassim, Takashi Yasuno,
Hiroshi Suzuki, Mohd Shahrieel Mohd Aras,
Ahmad Zaki Shukor, Hazriq Izzuan Jaafar and
Fairul Azni Jafar

Additional information is available at the end of the chapter

http://dx.doi.org/10.5772/intechopen.79886

Abstract

In general, a visually impaired person relies on guide canes in order to walk outside besides depending only on a tactile pavement as a warning and directional tool in order to avoid any obstructions or hazardous situations. However, still a lot of training is needed in order to recognize the tactile pattern, and it is quite difficult for persons who have recently become visually impaired. This chapter describes the development and evaluation of vision-based tactile paving detection method for visually impaired persons. Some experiments will be conducted on how it works to detect the tactile pavement and identify the shape of tactile pattern. In this experiment, a vision-based method is proposed by using MATLAB including the Arduino platform and speaker as guidance tools. The output of this system based on the result found from tactile detection in MATLAB then produces auditory output and notifies the visually impaired about the type of tactile detected. Consequently, the development of tactile pavement detection system can be used by visually impaired persons for easy detection and navigation purposes.

Keywords: tactile pavement, image recognition, navigation, guide cane, visually impaired person

1. Introduction

Accessibility is one of the main problems usually associated with disabled people [1]. Physically impaired people who are using the wheelchair have difficulties in going to their desired destination when they are faced with stairs, irregular roads, etc. The physically impaired people

© 2018 The Author(s). Licensee IntechOpen. This chapter is distributed under the terms of the Creative Commons Attribution License (http://creativecommons.org/licenses/by/3.0), which permits unrestricted use, distribution, and reproduction in any medium, provided the original work is properly cited. [cc] BY

IntechOpen

need a flattened surface or lift/barrier-free elevator to overcome the stairs or irregular surfaces. Besides, visually impaired people have problems of accessibility if there is no tactile pavement to guide them to their desired destination. The most significant problem or barrier is lack of infrastructure and safe mobility device for guiding the visually impaired in their everyday lives [2]. Hence, research has been carried out to develop and construct devices and infrastructure to guide them to their desired destination safely and without any collision [3].

The implementation of technology into the life of disabled people has the tendency to intensify their ability to have a more involved social life with the community around them. It could increase their quality of life and reduce the isolation problem of disabled people by increasing independence in their lives [4, 5]. This type of technology is called as assistive technology. Assistive technology has various meanings and purposes. As commonly known, assistive technology is a device or tool that can be used for supporting and helping disabled or elderly people. Besides, there are some categories of assistive technologies for different purposes such as rehabilitation, social assisting, etc. Some assistive technologies, which are developed to help disabled people, are well documented [6–9]. However, there are also some ethical issues that need to be considered while designing assistive technologies, which could benefit the disabled and elderly people [10–13].

In addition, the development of technologies that can help the visually impaired people has also emerged over the decades, which started from the Braille code typewriter to help them write and read. By using Braille with voice recognition system as the input interface, they can get to know the latest information around them. Currently, the usage of Braille is not only applied for typewriters, but there are also some research that have been done for implementing the Braille code on mobile phones, etc. [14–16], so that visually impaired people can use mobile phones as well as smartphones. Visually impaired and elderly people also need to be in line with the current technology because of the fast evolution in the communication era lately. There are also many software or applications inside the smartphone that can be used to help the visually impaired people, although they cannot see them. In addition, applying ubiquitous technologies such as in smartphones can make the visually impaired people understand and 'see' their surroundings [17, 18].

Besides, there are also some assistive technologies which are traditionally used by the visually impaired people such as a white cane, screen reader, etc. The concept of wearable assistive technology has also been drastically researched since the fabrication of a small device is possible now. The development of the wearable device also meets the requirements of the design challenges for assistive technology such as real-time guidance, portability, power limitations, appropriate interface, continuous availability, no dependence on infrastructure, low-cost solution, and minimal training. Therefore, disabled people such as visually impaired people are able to wear it while traveling outside [19–22].

In order to start the research endeavors, some literature reviews need to be conducted. This is because the current research needs to be understood first before the direction of the research is determined. Hence, some research studies have been reviewed, especially in assistive technology and rehabilitation study that aimed to help the visually impaired people to increase their quality of life (QOL) by leading more independent lives.

2. Navigation system

Navigation is a common problem for visually impaired people since they cannot travel by themselves. They cannot visually and freely decide the direction, in which they need to go since the information surrounding them cannot be obtained. Therefore, there are some researches and innovation works conducted to support and assist the visually impaired people to achieve self-independence when traveling at an indoor environment as well as outdoor environment. Therefore, some technologies need to be included in navigation systems in order for the system to be successfully executed. The technologies, which are required, include localization, path planning, error detection and correction, etc. Meanwhile, there are some localization technologies, which are focused on by some researchers. The localization technologies such as infrared data association (IrDA), radio frequency identification (RFID), near field communication (NFC), Bluetooth, light emitting method, Wi-Fi, etc. have been developed to help the visually impaired people to move while indoors with contextual information or sound navigation [23].

However, these methods have some limitations when used in outdoor environments. Therefore, the usage of global positioning system (GPS) devices can also help to guide the visually impaired people in an outdoor environment. GPS is a satellite-based system that provides the location of the GPS device by indicating the longitude and the latitude of the location. Some researchers have proved that the GPS cannot function properly in an indoor space and they have presented the solution of GPS by using the IrDA technology, which works as a detector to guide visually impaired people in indoor environment [24]. On the other hand, Lisa et al. combined the GPS that have developed in Drishti system and the ultrasonic sensors to be used for outdoor and indoor navigation [25]. However, one of the problems with GPS is accuracy; the accuracy of current GPS devices is about 5–10 m. The accuracy can also become worse when the measurement is done near tall buildings [26]. The measurement error is too big and very dangerous to be used by the visually impaired people since the location given by the GPS can guide them to the center of the road.

Furthermore, blind navigation system (BLI-NAV) is a navigation system, which consists of GPS receiver and path detector, designed for visually impaired people. Both devices are used to detect the user's location and determine the shortest route to the destination. Voice command is given throughout the travel. Path planning algorithm is used to determine the shortest distance from the start point to endpoint, together with the path detector. Moreover, the user is able to avoid obstacles while traveling [27]. This system gave better results in real-time performance and improved the efficiency of visually impaired travelers at an indoor environment.

On the other hand, pocket-PC–based electronic travel aid (ETA) is proposed to help visually impaired people to travel at an indoor environment. Pocket-PC will alert the user when they are near the obstacles through a warning audio [28]. An ultrasonic navigation device for visually impaired people has been designed. The microcontroller built in the device can guide the user in terms of which route should be taken through a speech output. Besides, the device helps to reduce navigation difficulties and detects obstacles using ultrasounds and vibrators. An ultrasonic range sensor is used to detect surrounding obstacles and electronic compass is used for direction navigation purpose. A stereoscopic sonar system is also used to detect the nearest obstacles and it feeds back to tell the user about the current location [29].

In addition, a visually impaired assistant navigation system that can help visually impaired people navigate independently at an indoor environment has also been developed [30]. The system provides localization by using a wireless mesh network. The server will do the path planning and then communicate using the wireless network with the portable mobile unit. The visually impaired people can give commands and receive the response from the server via audio signals using a headset with a microphone [31]. A proposed RFID technology in order to design the navigation system by providing information about their surroundings has also been developed. The system uses the RFID reader, which is mounted on one end of the stick to read the transponder tags that are installed on the tactile pavements [32]. At the same time, the research on RFID network can help to determine the shortest distance from the current location to the destination. Besides that, the system can help to find the way back if they lost their direction and recalculate a new path [33].

In addition, INSIGHT is an indoor navigation system to assist the visually impaired people to travel inside the buildings. The system uses RFID with Bluetooth technology to locate the user inside the buildings. Personal digital assistant (PDA) such as a mobile device is used to interact with the INSIGHT server and provide navigation information through voice commands. The zone that the user has walked on will be monitored by the system. The system will notify the user if the user travels in the wrong direction [34].

3. Development of navigation system for the visually impaired

In order to develop the navigation system, which will benefit the visually impaired people, a total navigation system that includes a path planning system, RFID detection system, and obstacle detection system is needed. However, in this chapter, the developed navigation system is only focused on the tactile pavement detection system using the image recognition method. Moreover, implementation of digital compass is used to guide visually impaired people when traveling [35]. **Figure 1** illustrates the system architecture by using ZigBee wireless networks for the communication between the server/laptop and the developed navigation device.

We developed the ZigBee network in order to connect and monitor the developed navigation device when the experiment is conducted. The ZigBee network acts as the center of data transferring between the navigation device and the server/laptop. The movement of user will be shown to the map processing system on the server/laptop respectively. Hence, the user's current position to the desired position will be displayed on the map based on a generated route. The map system then identifies the address of the target. Concurrently, the RFID reader/ writer module will read the RFID tags on the tactile paving or floor. The data of the RFID tags of the current position and the address is sent for map processing.

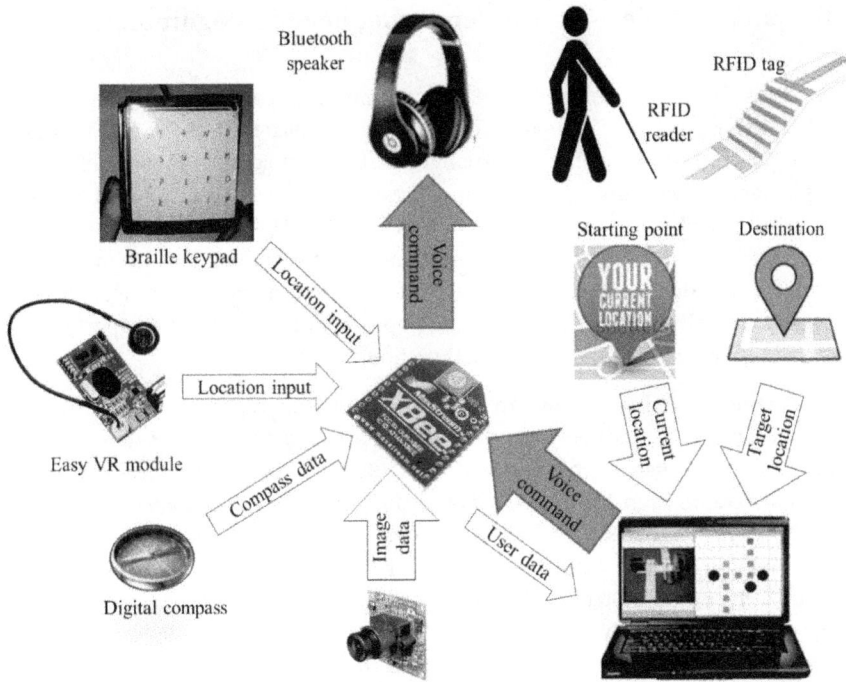

Figure 1. System architecture of developed navigation system including server/laptop.

Next, voice guidance commands will also be given based on the route, which has been generated, to the user through an earphone. The earphone connection is based on a Bluetooth connection. The server/laptop will send the voice guidance and user position will also be updated at the same time. Path recalculation will also be done again and voice guidance is produced if the user takes the wrong path from the recommended path. The benefit of the system is when the user needs to take a corner turning, the digital compass will compare the angle and ensure the user takes the corner effectively without hitting the nearby obstacles. The server receives data from ZigBee network and suggests mounting at fixed locations inside the buildings. The server must be updated and the information of the destinations and objects needs to be stored inside the database with respect to the map system.

In order to optimize the functionality of the developed navigation device for guiding the visually impaired people in the correct direction throughout the travel path, the experimental setup to evaluate the accuracy of the digital compass is set. The orientation or direction is attained by using a digital compass mounted on the developed electronic cane. The digital compass is connected to the Arduino microcontroller to obtain the analog signal and convert it back to the digital signal by using the onboard analog-digital converter (ADC). The digital signal will be displayed on the serial monitor of the Arduino microcontroller and the digital compass can be tuned accurately. The digital compass is fixed at the certain point where the RFID tag has been mounted to ensure the digital compass is always pointing to the north.

4. Tactile pavement detection system using image recognition

Figure 2 shows the system configuration between personal computer with MATLAB, web camera, Arduino microcontroller board, XBee transceiver, voice module WTS 020, and speaker in order to give auditory warning to visually impaired people after the implementation of vision-based tactile detection method. After a coding has been inserted into the Arduino microcontroller, it will be ready to receive signals from MATLAB, and then send commands to the voice module to play selected audio files. In order to produce auditory output, a voice module will be used to play the required audio file when commands are executed. **Figure 3** shows the actual hardware, which has been developed in order to validate the performances of the proposed vision-based tactile pavement detection system.

From the illustration, which is shown in **Figure 3**, a web camera is mounted on the center of the electronic cane. A distance between the webcam to the tactile paving is about 50 cm. The web camera is connected to the personal computer, which has been installed with the MATLAB software through XBee wireless communication. The personal computer will process the image, which has been captured through the web camera by using the proposed tactile pavement detection system. After the shape of the tactile pavement has been successfully determined by the proposed tactile pavement detection system, two types of voice guide will be given, which are WARNING and DIRECTION, through user's Bleutooth headphone. The result of the detection will be sent through the XBee transceiver to guide the cane's transceiver in order to activate the voice module. The voice guidance will be given through Bluetooth wireless communication.

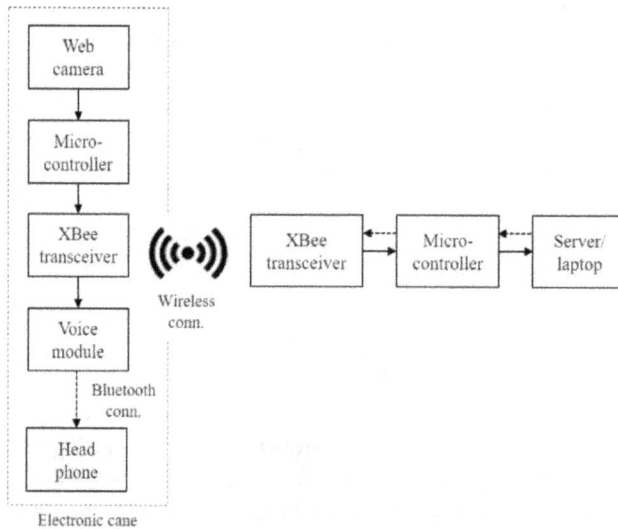

Figure 2. System configuration for vision-based tactile paving detection system.

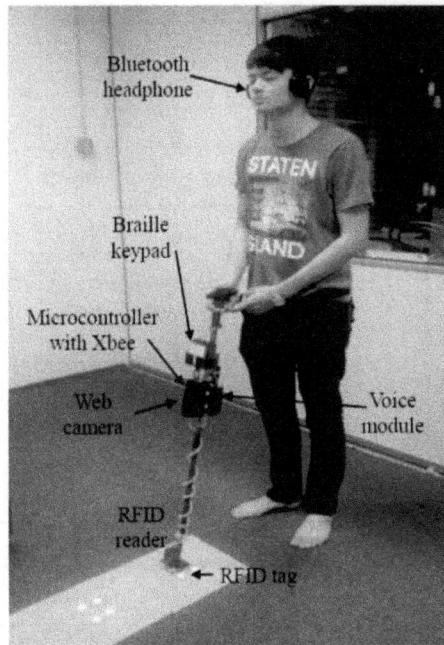

Figure 3. Developed blind navigation system hardware.

This vision-based system consists of five main phases. The first part is to input the image containing the tactile pavement with the warning tactile and directional tactile. The second part is the preprocessing of the input images, which includes the filtering of the noises for the tactile detection in the image. The third part is to extract and determine the area and perimeter of the connected components detected in the image. The fourth part is to determine the metric for the connected components by using the area calculation algorithm of the detected components. The last part is to produce the accurate audio output to the visually impaired people. A process flowchart regarding the overall process of this system is shown in **Figure 4**.

4.1. Input image

A webcam/camera will be used to capture the image that contains the pattern of tactile pavement. It will be loaded into MATLAB for further preprocessing to successfully detect any possible tactile shapes. **Figure 5(a)** and **(b)** shows the images of tactile paving, which are warning tactile and directional tactile.

4.2. Preprocessing

This phase of the whole process is to filter the image actually required to be detected in MATLAB. Several steps are shown in **Figure 4** in preprocessing, which are important to achieve the goal of the vision-based system.

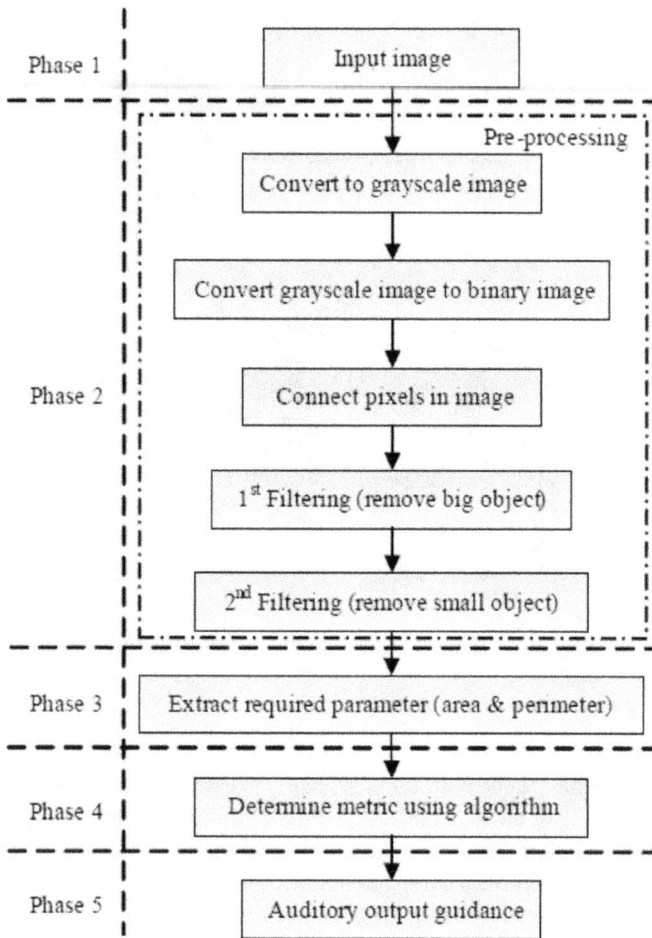

Figure 4. Overall process flowchart for vision-based tactile pavement detection system.

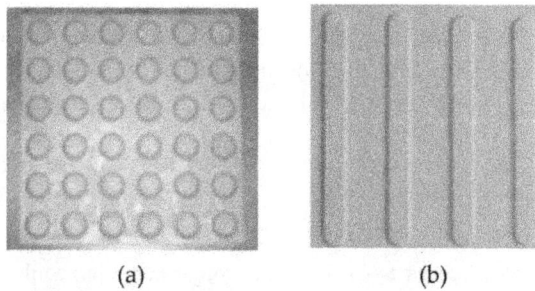

Figure 5. Input tactile image. (a) Warning tactile and (b) direction tactile.

4.3. Color image to grayscale image

The previous image is an RGB image, which is a colored image. The brightness levels of the red (R), green (G), and blue (B) components are each represented as a number from decimal 0 to 255. Therefore, the RGB image has to be converted to black-and-white image for the ease of processing. The lightness of the gray color is directly proportional to the number representing the brightness levels of the primary colors. Black is represented by value for each R, G, and B is 0. Meanwhile, white is represented by value of each R, G, and B is 1. The converted grayscale image is shown in **Figure 6**.

4.4. Grayscale image to binary image

This process will change the grayscale image to a binary image, which is an image with only black and white pixels in it. **Figure 6(a)** shows the grayscale image after the conversion process. The pixel values that exist in this format of image are only 0, which is black in color, and 1, which is white in color. **Figure 6(b)** shows the resulting image of the binary image after it has been through the threshold method when the threshold has been set to the value of 0.5.

4.5. Connecting pixels in image

In this phase, preprocessing is used to identify the connected components inside the binary image. **Figure 7** shows the connected components algorithm, which is applied in order to identify the connected components by using a group of binary symbols. After the connected components have been identified, the next process is to fill the "holes" inside any connected pixels in the image automatically using MATLAB, in an attempt to make the connected pixels look more obvious. Therefore, further detecting processes for the tactile shapes can be performed easily. The processed image in which the "holes" have been filled with white color is shown in **Figure 8**.

4.6. First round of image filtering

This process has been implemented to remove all objects that are connected to the edge, in which these noises could cause problems for tactile detection in the image. Furthermore, pixels

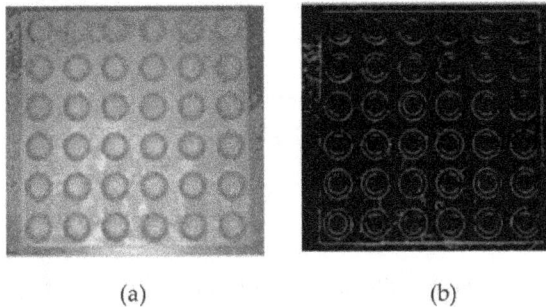

(a)   (b)

Figure 6. Image conversion process. (a) Grayscale image and (b) binary image.

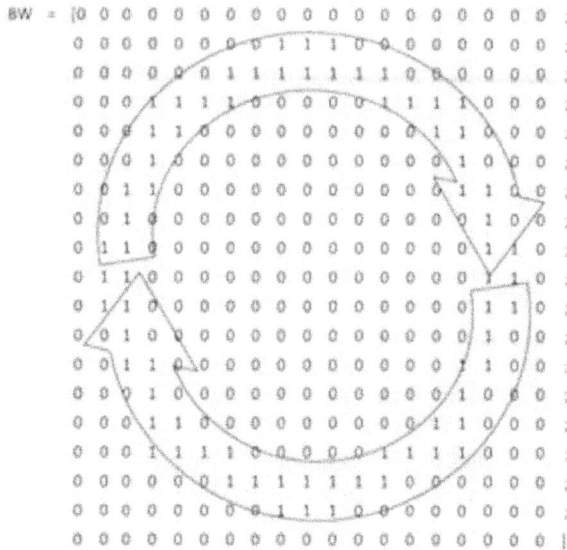

Figure 7. Connected components algorithm.

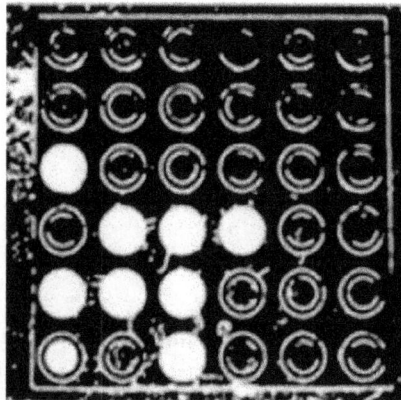

Figure 8. Image with filled holes inside connected components.

that are connected to the edge are more than likely to be useless in gaining any information that is required, therefore removing them would work as filtering. **Figure 9** shows the image with a cleared border.

4.7. Second round of image filtering

As shown in **Figure 9(a)**, there are still far too many noises present in the image, even after the first round of image filtering. Therefore, another method has been implemented to filter the image of the noises even more. This method is to set a threshold value for the pixel size, and anything that has a pixel value below the threshold value will be removed. **Figure 9(b)** shows the image after it has removed all components that have a pixel value of less than 1000 pixel^2.

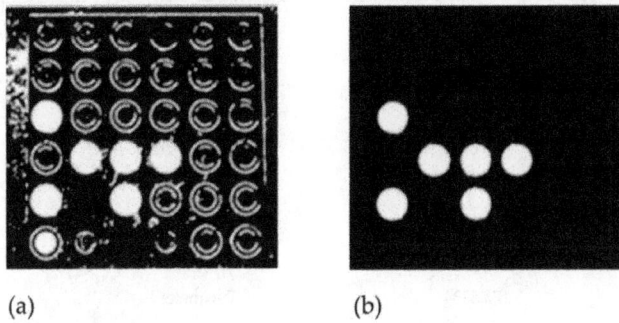

(a)   (b)

Figure 9. Filtering process. (a) First round filtered image and (b) second round filtered image.

4.8. Extract required parameters from connected components

In this phase, after the image is filtered by preprocessing, some parameters are required from the connected pixels/components that are left. The parameters required by the tactile detection algorithm are area and perimeter of the left image. A function in MATLAB will be used to determine these required parameters. **Figure 10** shows the pieces of area, which is recognized, and each of the parameters found by the function on the connected pixels is shown in **Table 1(a)–(f)**.

4.9. Determining the metric

This phase will be the main part that will decide whether the connected components/pixels in the image are the potential image containing tactile or not. The metric m is determined by using Eq. (1).

$$m = \frac{4\pi A}{p^2} \tag{1}$$

where m indicates the metric, A indicates the area, and p indicates the perimeter. Therefore, it is important to obtain the required parameters, which are the area and perimeter of the connected pixels before this phase. MATLAB will calculate the metric from the parameters obtained earlier using Eq. (1). **Table 2** shows the result of the metrics of the connected components/pixels.

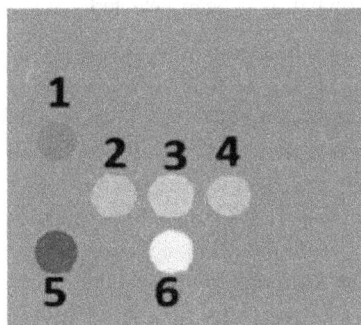

Figure 10. Parameters (area, perimeter, centroid) of the connected pixels.

(a) Parameter for no. 1		(d) Parameter for no. 4	
Area	1919	Area	1951
Centroid	[146.1730, 176.4815]	Centroid	[348.2952, 242.4567]
Perimeter	163.7317	Perimeter	165.6812
(b) Parameter for no. 2		(e) Parameter for no. 5	
Area	1980	Area	1984
Centroid	[213.070, 242.8086]	Centroid	[144.9057, 311.9995]
Perimeter	173.8234	Perimeter	170.6102
(c) Parameter for no. 3		(f) Parameter for no. 6	
Area	1988	Area	1993
Centroid	[280.6459, 242.7938]	Centroid	[280.9910, 310.4752]
Perimeter	177.6812	Perimeter	173.0955

Table 1. Metric table.

No.	1	2	3	4	5	6
Area	1919	1980	1988	1951	1984	1993
Metric	0.899	0.823	0.791	0.893	0.857	0.836

Table 2. Calculation results of metric for each area.

4.10. Producing auditory output based on metric

After the metric for each connected component/pixel has been calculated, the "shape" for each will be determined. In the results, it is proven that the connected pixels which have metric values in the range of 0.85–1.0 will most likely be a circle, representing the warning tactile. In contrast, the connected pixels that have metric values in the range of 0.15–0.30 will most likely be a bar, which represents the directional tactile. **Figure 11(a)** and **(b)** shows the results of the metric for warning and directional tactile images. After the results of metric values have been calculated, the system will then send a signal to the auditory output system, and notify the visually impaired people about what have been detected.

Figure 12 shows the overall process flow system hardware for the auditory output. In this case, when the warning tactile has been detected (metric value in range from 0.85 to 1.0) in MATLAB, MATLAB will send a signal to the voice module to have an auditory output saying WARNING via Arduino microcontroller, and if the directional tactile has been detected (metric value in range from 0.15 to 0.30), the auditory output would be DIRECTION. Prior to sending signal to the voice module from MATLAB via Arduino microcontroller, a serial communication between MATLAB and Arduino must first be made. After the serial communication has been established, only then will Arduino microcontroller be able to receive any signals from MATLAB when the command is being given.

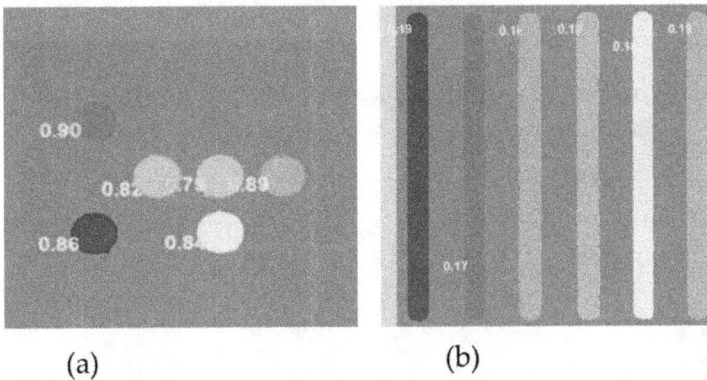

(a)   (b)

Figure 11. Final image results. (a) Warning tactile and (b) direction tactile.

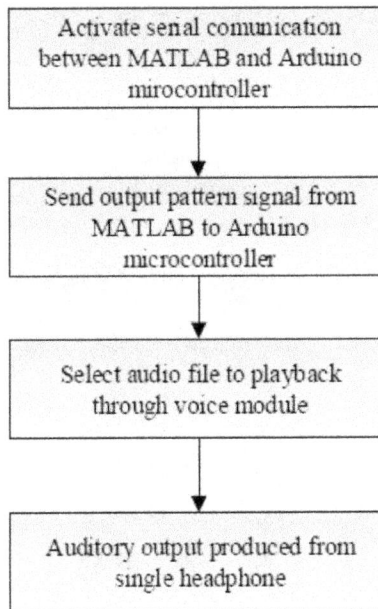

Figure 12. System hardware control flowchart.

After the metric has been determined, a certain signal will be sent to the Arduino microcontroller, where coding is already uploaded to the Arduino microcontroller board beforehand through the Arduino I/O interface. There are three cases where the metric values are in the range 0.15–0.30, 0.85–1.0 and the range other than the mentioned metric values. For example, when the metric values of range 0.15–0.30 are found, MATLAB will send a signal to indicate DIRECTION, and Arduino microcontroller will receive it, and execute the next command. It is the same for two other cases, where 'WARNING' voice signal will be sent if metric values of range 0.85 to 1.0, while 'ERROR' voice signal will be sent if none of this two metric range are determined.

5. Results and discussions

In order to validate the effectiveness of the developed vision-based tactile detection method, an experiment is conducted to recognize a variety of shapes by using the proposed detection

Tactile image	Detection metric	Result
		Circle (0.9–1.0)
		Bar (0.15–0.3)
		Eclipse (0.82)
		Square (0.79)
		Triangle (0.58)
		Diamond (0.68)

Table 3. Detection results of variety of shapes.

algorithm. This experiment is conducted to prove that the proposed detection algorithm can compare different shapes such as circle, bar, eclipse, square, triangle, and diamond. These shapes have been captured through web camera and downloaded from Internet. A metric calculation is used to detect the shapes. The metric in the coding works by calculating any connected component's area and perimeter in a binary image after preprocessing, and then computing it using Eq. (1). After the metric has worked on the connected components, it will give a certain range of values for different shapes detected.

Table 3 shows the detection results of a variety of shapes by using the proposed tactile detection algorithm. From Table 3 results, the range of the metric value for each shape is confirmed by using the vision-based tactile detection algorithm. These metric values will be the benchmark value for each shape in order to differentiate the image shape. However, there are some shapes, which are having similar metric values such as circle, eclipse, and square. These analysis results will be used to improvise the current detection algorithm, making the system better and more robust to different types of detection environment of the tactile paving.

The detection of these various shapes will be used in order to recognize and differentiate the different shapes of items such as leaf, construction pavement, box, various shapes of papers/ garbage, etc. The detection of these various shapes will be used in order to recognize and differentiate the different shapes of items such as leaf, construction pavement, box, various shapes of papers/ garbage, etc. which usually covered the tactile pavement in real environment. A higher accuracy of detection system is needed to give higher reliability and give confidence to the visually impaired person when using the tactile pavement detection system to travel safely. Therefore, the result of the proposed detection system is very important for the blind navigation system, which is proposed in Figure 1.

6. Conclusions

In this chapter, the performance of a developed vision-based tactile detection algorithm, which was used to recognize the shape of tactile pavement for navigation purpose, was evaluated. The vision-based tactile detection algorithm was proposed and the experimental study on effectiveness of the detection algorithm by using five phases, which are load image, preprocessing, parameters extraction, metric calculation, and auditory output, was conducted. The proposed vision-based tactile paving detection system was also confirmed to be functioned in order to differentiate variety of shapes such as circle, bar, eclipse, square, triangle, and diamond. All the metric values could be applied as benchmark metric values for the next step of development of visually impaired navigation system.

Acknowledgements

This research is a collaboration project between Graduate School of Advanced Technology and Science, Tokushima University, and Centre for Robotics and Industrial Automation, Universiti Teknikal Malaysia Melaka.

Author details

Anuar Bin Mohamed Kassim[1]*, Takashi Yasuno[1], Hiroshi Suzuki[1],
Mohd Shahrieel Mohd Aras[2], Ahmad Zaki Shukor[2], Hazriq Izzuan Jaafar[2] and
Fairul Azni Jafar[2]

*Address all correspondence to: anuar@utem.edu.my

1 Graduate School of Advanced Technology and Science, Tokushima University, Tokushima, Japan

2 Faculty of Electrical Engineering, Centre for Robotics and Industrial Automation, Universiti Teknikal Malaysia Melaka, Melaka, Malaysia

References

[1] Foley A, Ferri BA. Technology for people, not disabilities: Ensuring access and inclusion. Journal of Research in Special Educational Needs. 2012;**12**(4):192-200

[2] Bujacz M, Baranski P, Moranski M, Materka A. Remote mobility and navigation aid for the visually disabled. In: 7th International Conference on Disability, Virtual Reality and Associated Technologies with Artabilitation; 8-11 September 2008; Portugal. pp. 263-270

[3] Strumillo P. Electronic interfaces aiding the visually impaired in environmental access, mobility and navigation. In: 2010 3rd International Conference on Human Systems Interactions; 13-15 May 2010; Rzeszow. Poland. pp. 17-24

[4] Lamourex EL, Hassell JB, Keeffe JE. The determinants of participation in activities of daily living in people with impaired vision. American Journal of Ophthalmology. 2004;**137**(2): 265-270

[5] Scherer MJ. Living in the State of Stuck: How Assistive Technology Impacts the Lives of People with Disabilities. Fourth ed. Cambridge, MA: Brookline Books; 2005

[6] Leventhal JD. Assistive devices for people who are blind or have visual impairments. In: Assistive Technology. Gaithersburg, MD: Aspen Publishers; 1996. pp. 125-143

[7] Cheverst K, Clarke K, Dewsbury G, Hemmings T, Kember S, Rodden T, Rouncefield M. Designing assistive technologies for medication regimes in care settings. Universal Access in the Information Society (UAIS). 2003;**2**(3):235-242

[8] Steel EJ, De Witte LP. Advances in European assistive technology service delivery and recommendations for further improvement. Technology and Disability. July 2011;**23**(3): 131-138

[9] Mountain G. Using the evidence to develop quality assistive technology services. Journal of Integrated Care. 2004;**12**(1):19-26

[10] Sharkey A, Sharkey N. Granny and the robots: Ethical issues in robot care for the elderly. Ethics and Information Technology. 2012;**14**(1):27-40

[11] Perry J, Beyer S. Ethical issues around telecare: The views of people with intellectual disabilities and people with dementia. Journal of Assistive Technologies. 2012;**6**(1):71-75

[12] Dewsbury G, Clarke K, Hughes J, Rouncefield M, Sommerville I. Growing older digitally: Designing technology for older people. In: Inclusive Design for Society and Business; 25-28 March 2003; London. London: Helen Hamlyn Institute; pp. 57-64

[13] Leonard VK, Jacko JA, Pizzimenti JJ. An investigation of handheld device use by older adults with age-related macular degeneration. Behaviour & Information Technology. 2006;**25**(4):313-332

[14] Jayant C, Acuario C, Johnson W A, Hollier J, Ladner R E. VBraille: Haptic Braille perception using a touch-screen and vibration on mobile phones. In: 12th International ACM SIGACCESS Conference on Computers and Accessibility (ASSETS); 25-27 October 2010; Orlando, FL, USA. pp. 295-296

[15] Azenkot S, Fortuna E. Improving public transit usability for blind and deaf-blind people by connecting a braille display to a smartphone. In: 12th International ACM SIGACCESS Conference on Computers and Accessibility (ASSETS'10); 25-27 October 2010; Orlando, FL, USA. pp. 317-318

[16] Johnson KL, Dudgeon B, Amtmann D. Assistive technology in rehabilitation. Physical Medicine and Rehabilitation Clinics of North America. 1997;**8**(2):389-403

[17] Wang H, Zhang Y, Cao J. Ubiquitous computing environments and its usage access control. In: First International Conference on Scalable Information Systems (INFOSCALE '06); May 30-June 1 2006; p. 10

[18] Vergados DD. Service personalization for assistive living in a mobile ambient healthcare-networked environment. Personal and Ubiquitous Computing. 2010;**14**(6):575-590

[19] Dakopoulos D, Bourbakis NG. Wearable obstacle avoidance electronic travel aids for blind: A survey. IEEE Transactions on Systems, Man, and Cybernetic, Part C: Applications and Reviews. 2010;**40**(1):25-35

[20] Zhang J, Lip CW, Ong SK, Nee AYC. Development of a shoe-mounted assistive user interface for navigation. International Journal of Sensor Networks. 2012;**9**(1):3-12

[21] Tsai D, Morley JW, Suaning GJ, Lovell NH. A wearable real-time image processor for a vision prosthesis. Computer Methods and Programs in Biomedicine. 2009;**95**:258-269

[22] Cardin S, Thalmann D, Vexo F. A wearable system for mobility improvement of visually impaired people. The Visual Computer. February 2007;**23**(2):109-118

[23] Interface. Research: Latest GPS and Indoor Measurement. Japan: CQ Publisher; 2013 in Japanese

[24] Wise E, Li B, Gallagher T, Dempster AG, Rizos C, Ramsey-Stewart E, Woo D. Indoor navigation for the blind and vision impaired: Where are we and where are we going? In: 2012 International Conference on Indoor Positioning and Indoor Navigation (IPIN); 13-15 November 2012; pp. 1-7

[25] Ran L, Helal S, Moore S. Drishti: An integrated indoor/outdoor blind navigation system and service. In: Proceedings of 2nd IEEE Ann. Conf. on Pervasive Computing and Communications (PerCom 2004); March 2004; pp. 23-30

[26] Sarfraz M, Rizvi SAJ. Indoor navigational aid system for the visually impaired. Second International Conference on Geometric Modeling and Imaging (GMAI). 2007:127-132

[27] Santhosh SS, Sasiprabha T, Jeberson R. BLI-NAV embedded navigation system for blind people. Recent Advances in Space Technology Services and Climate Change (RSTSCC). 2010:277-282

[28] Choudhury MH, Aguerrevere D, Barreto AB. A pocket-PC based navigational aid for blind individuals. In: 2004 IEEE Symposium on Virtual Environments, Human-Computer Interfaces and Measurement Systems (VECIMS). 2004. pp. 43-48

[29] Bousbia-Salah M, Redjati A, Fezari M, Bettayeb M. An ultrasonic navigation system for blind people. In: 2007 IEEE International Conference on Signal Processing and Communications ICSPC. 2007. pp. 1003-1006

[30] Shamsi M, Al-Qutayri M, Jeedella J. Blind assistant navigation system. In: 2011 1st Middle East Conference on Biomedical Engineering (MECBME). 2011. pp. 163-166

[31] Chumkamon S, Tuvaphanthaphiphat P, Keeratiwintakorn P. A blind navigation system using RFID for indoor environments. In: 5th International Conference on Electrical Engineering/Electronics, Computer, Telecommunications and Information Technology. Vol. 2. 2008. pp. 765-768

[32] Kassim AM, Jaafar HI, Azam MA, Abas N, Yasuno T. Design and development of navigation system by using RFID technology. In: 3rd IEEE International Conference on System Engineering and Technology (ICSET). 2013. pp. 258-262

[33] Kassim AM, Shukor AZ, Zhi CX, Yasuno T. Exploratory study on navigation system for visually impaired people. Australian Journal of Basic and Applied Sciences. 2013;7(14): 211-217

[34] Ganz A, Gandhi SR, Wilson C, Mullett G. INSIGHT: RFID and bluetooth enabled automated space for the blind and visually impaired. In: IEEE International Conference of Engineering in Medicine and Biology Society. 2010. pp. 331-334

[35] Kassim AM, Yasuno T, Suzuki H, Jaafar HI, Aras MSM. Indoor navigation system based on passive RFID transponder with digital compass for visually impaired people. International Journal of Advanced Computer Science and Applications (IJACSA). 2016;7(2):604-611

Machine Navigation Systems

Micro-Inertial-Aided High-Precision Positioning Method for Small-Diameter PIG Navigation

Lianwu Guan, Xu Xu, Yanbin Gao, Fanming Liu, Hanxiao Rong, Meng Wang and Aboelmagd Noureldin

Additional information is available at the end of the chapter

http://dx.doi.org/10.5772/intechopen.80343

Abstract

Pipeline leakage or explosion has caused huge economic losses, polluted the environments and threatened the safety of civilian's lives and assets, which even caused negative influences to the society greatly. Fortunately, pipeline inspection gauge (PIG) could accomplish the pipeline defect (corrosions, cracks, grooves, etc.) inspection effectively and meanwhile to localize these defects precisely by navigation sensors. The results are utilized for pipeline integrity management (PIM) and pipeline geographic information system construction. Generally, the urban underground pipeline presents with small-diameter and complicated-distribution properties, which are of great challenges for the pipeline defects positioning by PIG. This chapter focuses on in-depth research of the high-precision positioning method for small-diameter PIG navigation. In the beginning, the problems and system errors statement of MEMS SINS-based PIG are analyzed step by step. Then, the pipeline junction (PJ) identification method based on fast orthogonal search (FOS) is studied. After that, a PIG positioning system that comprises of micro-inertial/AGM/odometer/PJ is proposed, and also the application mechanism of extended Kalman filter and its smoothing technology on PIG navigation system is researched to improve the overall positioning precision for the small-diameter PIG. Finally, the proposed methods and research conclusions are verified by the indoor wheel robot simulation platform.

Keywords: micro-inertial navigation, small-diameter PIG, pipeline junction, fast orthogonal search, extended Kalman filter and smoothing technology

IntechOpen

© 2018 The Author(s). Licensee IntechOpen. This chapter is distributed under the terms of the Creative Commons Attribution License (http://creativecommons.org/licenses/by/3.0), which permits unrestricted use, distribution, and reproduction in any medium, provided the original work is properly cited. (cc) BY

1. Introduction

Pipeline is one of the useful transportation tools to deliver the gases or liquids from the starting point to the different user destinations effectively and safely. For example, in Canada, 97% of the raw oil and gas production is transported by pipeline according to the Canadian energy pipelines association (CEPA) data [1]. Moreover, the total length of routed pipelines used for oil and gas transportation has exceeded 600,000 km in North America [2]. However, when pipeline is operated over its designed life expectancy, and also when meets with natural disasters or human damages, the pipeline is easily broken and causes the leakage of gas or oil [3]. The leakage would lead to the environmental pollution, explosion, even lives in danger especially when the leakage or explosion occurred in urban areas with high populations. Therefore, the detection as well as positioning of pipeline defects by pipeline inspection gauge (PIG) is of great importance to fulfill the pipeline integrity management (PIM) and pipeline geographic information system (GIS) construction.

Generally, the pipeline detection methods include in-pipeline inspection and outer-pipeline inspection. But depending on the requirements of transportation and the land-usage reasons, almost most of the pipeline is buried underground. That is to say, it is extremely difficult, time-consuming, and expensive to reach and inspect the pipeline from its outside. Therefore, PIG is designed to inspect the existed or potential pipeline defects in the inner or outer surface of pipeline by driven with the gas or liquid in the pipeline, which could improve the safety rate of operational pipeline to be 99.99% under related regulations [4]. In addition, PIG is usually equipped with various electronic devices to record the physical data about the pipeline situation and to analyze them offline.

Pipeline defect inspection and localization are two main missions for a PIG system [5]. Magnetic flux leakage (MFL) and ultrasonic (UT) are the main inspection technologies that is usually used to detect the pipeline defects when installing in the PIG [6]. The information provided by these technologies need to be synchronized with the positioning technology to obtain pipeline defect coordinates accurately for PIM and GIS construction. Generally, inertial navigation system (INS) is to be more suitable for this purpose than GPS because the satellite signal from GPS is completely interrupted by the Earth and the steel-structured pipeline. Moreover, the 3D orthogonal accelerations and 3D orthogonal angular rates of PIG are measured by inertial measurement unit (IMU), and these measurements are adopted to determine the coordinates of pipeline centerline by INS mechanization [7]. Meanwhile, the horizontal and vertical pipeline curvatures could also be calculated to expose the potential pipeline bend or displacement [8]. A typical PIG that carries the inspection sensors with strapdown INS (SINS) is shown in **Figure 1**.

Different from the navigation in other applications, the motions of PIG inside the inspected pipeline are comprised of its longitudinal rotation motion (rolling) and the regular traveling motion along the pipeline longitudinal direction [9]. The PIG rolling motion could improve its go-through capability in some wax obstacle or heavy sludge areas at the bottom part of the pipeline. Meanwhile, the inspection capability for the pipeline inspection sensors on potential pipeline defects is improved significantly by PIG rolling motion. Furthermore, the rolling motion enhances the positioning precision of SINS-based PIG navigation, and therefore improves the

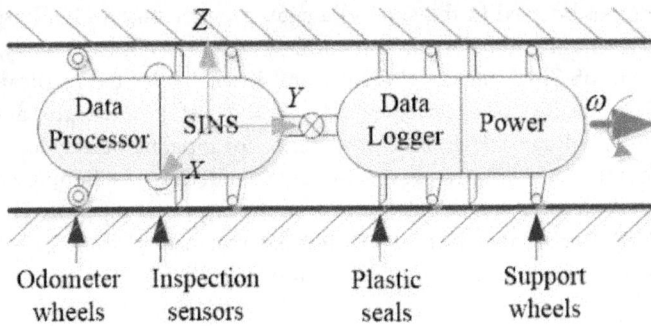

Figure 1. A typical PIG for inner-pipeline inspection.

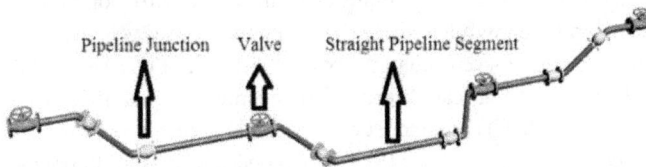

Figure 2. A typical pipeline with PJs and valves.

pipeline defect positioning precision that minimizes the costs and labor involved for PIM and GIS building for the inspected pipeline.

A normal pipeline is demonstrated in **Figure 2**; the pipeline junction (PJ) is usually used to connect the two adjacent straight pipeline segments (SPSs) and also connect the pipeline to the valve. The azimuth and pitch angles of the PIG in each SPS are constant because the cylinder-shaped PIG is constrained by pipeline in the horizontal and vertical directions [10]. Hence, the detection of the PJs could provide azimuth and pitch angle updates and improve the positioning precision for SINS-based PIG.

This chapter aims to have an in-depth research of its high-precision positioning method for the small-diameter PIG navigation. At the beginning, the unique movement characteristic of PIG is analyzed in Section 2. Then, the PJ detection method based on fast orthogonal search (FOS) is studied to implement the PJ detection accurately in Section 3. After that, a PIG positioning system that comprises of micro-inertial/AGM/odometer/PJ is proposed and also the application mechanism of extended Kalman filter (EKF) and its smoothing technology on the PIG positioning system is researched to improve the overall positioning precision for the small-diameter PIG in Section 4. The proposed methods and research experiments are performed in Section 5. Finally, the conclusions are summarized in Section 6.

2. The MEMS SINS-based PIG

Currently, most of the PIG navigation system is comprised of fiber optic gyroscope (FOG)-based SINS when the diameter of pipeline is over 12." However, due to the volume constrain, the FOG SINS cannot be used in the small-diameter pipeline-based PIG. Fortunately, with the rapid development of microelectromechanical-system (MEMS) technology, the position-ing precision of MEMS SINS improved greatly and it accelerates the application of MEMS SINS in small-diameter PIG. Therefore, considering the cost, size, weight, and power con-sumption, the small-volume MEMS SINS is superior for pipeline defects localization when its diameter is less than 12" [11]. However, the pipeline defects positioning error of MEMS SINS is divergent with the distance enlargement of the inspected pipeline. The main reason is the error of MEMS inertial sensors is much greater than that of the usually used FOG inertial sensors-based pipeline navigation application [12].

2.1. The problem statement of MEMS SINS-based PIG

At present, the rear part of PIG is symmetrically installed with odometers to measure its longitudinal velocity and meanwhile reduce the slippage-induced velocity error, which is used for the reduction of the time-accumulated error of SINS in PIG. Meanwhile, zero-velocity updates in both lateral and vertical directions of cylinder-shaped PIG are provided by its nonholonomic constraint (NHC) characteristic. Hence, there are 3D continuous velocity updates for SINS of PIG. Moreover, the 3D coordinates of pipeline valves and above-ground markers (AGMs) are provided by DGPS, which are used for 3D sporadic coordinate updates for SINS of PIG [13]. Nevertheless, the continuous 3D velocity and sporadic 3D coordinate updates cannot satisfy the surveying precision requirements in small-volume MEMS SINS-based pipeline navi-gation system in small diameter pipeline.

Apart from the velocity and position errors, the attitude error (pitch error δp, roll error δr, and azimuth error δA) also degrades the positioning precision of MEMS SINS-based PIG. The change rates of PIG horizontal velocity errors $\delta \dot{v}_n$ and $\delta \dot{v}_e$ are given by [14]:

$$\begin{cases} \delta \dot{v}_n = -f_u \delta p + f_e \delta A + \delta f_n \\ \delta \dot{v}_e = -f_u \delta r + f_n \delta A + \delta f_e \end{cases} \tag{1}$$

where, δf_e and δf_n denote accelerometer biases in Earth east and north directions. f_e, f_n, and f_u denote acceleration components in Earth east, north, and up directions.

In Eq. (1), the value of f_u is close to local Earth gravity and it is much bigger than f_e and f_n in PIG navigation application. Hence, the pitch and roll errors of SINS in PIG are tightly coupled with the corresponding horizontal velocity errors, and the 3D velocity errors of PIG are observable by odometers and NHC. Therefore, the azimuth error of SINS in PIG is not observable, while the pitch and roll errors are observable. The horizontal position errors of SINS in PIG are obtained by twice integration on the change rate of azimuth-error-induced horizontal velocity errors [14]:

$$\begin{cases} \delta \dot{v}_{n2} = f_e \delta A \\ \delta \dot{v}_{e2} = -f_n \delta A \end{cases} \rightarrow \begin{cases} \delta P_{n2}(t_k) = \delta P_{n2}(t_{k-1}) + v_e \delta A \Delta t \\ \delta P_{e2}(t_k) = \delta P_{e2}(t_{k-1}) - v_n \delta A \Delta t \end{cases} \tag{2}$$

where $\varDelta\delta P_{n2}$ and $\varDelta\delta P_{e2}$ are the azimuth-error-induced horizontal position errors. They are also related to PIG horizontal velocities v_e and v_n, and the time interval $\varDelta t$. More intuitively, when PIG travels with 1 m/s in horizontal velocity, and 1° in azimuth error, the position error that caused by azimuth error is about 89 m in 1 h of PIG navigation. Therefore, to correct the azimuth error is an important way to enhance the navigation precision of SINS-based PIG.

At present, azimuth sensors, like camera, magnetometer, and optical navigation sensor are usually adopted to improve the measurement precision of azimuth, but both the cost and weight of PIG would increase. Moreover, their measurement precision is also severely degraded by the pipeline application [8]. So, it is not viable for these sensors to be applied to correct the azimuth error of PIG accurately. However, it is worth noting that the routed pipeline is connected by fixed-length SPS via PJ. The cylinder-shaped PIG makes the azimuth and pitch maintain constant from the beginning to the end of each SPS. Therefore, the azimuth and pitch mechanized by SINS at the beginning of SPS are usually used as updates in the corresponding SPS. Consequently, the PJ detection result provides azimuth and pitch updates for MEMS SINS, and the PJ detection would be analyzed in Section 3.

2.2. The system error model of MEMS SINS-based PIG

For the SINS-based PIG navigation system, the system error model is given by [14]:

$$\delta\dot{x} = \begin{bmatrix} F_{11} & F_{12} & 0_{3*3} & 0_{3*3} & 0_{3*3} \\ F_{21} & F_{22} & F_{23} & 0_{3*3} & R_b^n \\ F_{31} & F_{32} & F_{33} & R_b^n & 0_{3*3} \\ 0_{3*3} & 0_{3*3} & 0_{3*3} & F_{44} & 0_{3*3} \\ 0_{3*3} & 0_{3*3} & 0_{3*3} & 0_{3*3} & F_{55} \end{bmatrix} \delta x + Gw \tag{3}$$

where

$$F_{11} = \begin{bmatrix} 0 & 0 & -\dot{\phi}/(R_M + h) \\ \dot{\lambda}\tan\phi & 0 & -\dot{\lambda}/(R_N + h) \\ 0 & 0 & 0 \end{bmatrix}, F_{23} = \begin{bmatrix} 0 & f_u & -f_n \\ -f_u & 0 & f_e \\ f_n & -f_e & 0 \end{bmatrix},$$

$$F_{12} = \begin{bmatrix} 0 & \dfrac{1}{R_M + h} & 0 \\ \dfrac{1}{(R_N + h)\cos\phi} & 0 & 0 \\ 0 & 0 & 1 \end{bmatrix}, F_{32} = \begin{bmatrix} 0 & \dfrac{1}{R_M + h} & 0 \\ \dfrac{-1}{R_N + h} & 0 & 0 \\ \dfrac{-\tan\phi}{R_N + h} & 0 & 0 \end{bmatrix},$$

$$F_{21} = \begin{bmatrix} 2\omega_e\left(v_u\sin\phi + v_n\cos\phi\right) + \dot{\lambda}v_n/\cos\phi & 0 & 0 \\ -2\omega_e v_e\cos\phi - \dot{\lambda}v_e/\cos\phi & 0 & 0 \\ -2\omega_e v_e\sin\phi & 0 & 2g/R_N \end{bmatrix},$$

$$F_{22} = \begin{bmatrix} (v_n \tan\phi - v_u)/(R_N + h) & (2\omega_e + \dot{\lambda})\sin\phi & -(2\omega_e + \dot{\lambda})\cos\phi \\ -2(\omega_e + \dot{\lambda})\sin\phi & -v_u/(R_M + h) & -\dot{\phi} \\ 2(\omega_e + \dot{\lambda})\cos\phi & 2\dot{\phi} & 0 \end{bmatrix},$$

$$F_{31} = \begin{bmatrix} 0 & 0 & -\dot{\lambda}/(R_M + h) \\ \omega_e \sin\phi & 0 & \dot{\lambda}\cos\phi/(R_N + h) \\ -\omega_e \cos\phi - \dot{\lambda}/(R_N + h)\cos\phi & 0 & \dot{\lambda}\sin\phi/(R_N + h) \end{bmatrix}, F_{44} = \begin{bmatrix} -\beta_{wx} & 0 & 0 \\ 0 & -\beta_{wy} & 0 \\ 0 & 0 & -\beta_{wz} \end{bmatrix},$$

$$F_{33} = \begin{bmatrix} 0 & (\omega_e + \dot{\lambda})\sin\phi & -(\omega_e + \dot{\lambda})\cos\phi \\ -(\omega_e + \dot{\lambda})\sin\phi & 0 & -\dot{\phi} \\ (\omega_e + \dot{\lambda})\cos\phi & \dot{\phi} & 0 \end{bmatrix}, F_{55} = \begin{bmatrix} -\beta_{fx} & 0 & 0 \\ 0 & -\beta_{fy} & 0 \\ 0 & 0 & -\beta_{fz} \end{bmatrix}$$

and, ϕ and λ are local latitude and longitude, $\dot{\phi} = v_n/(R_M + h)$, $\dot{\lambda} = v_e/(R_M + h)\cos\phi$. R_M, R_N, and h are meridian radius, normal radius, and geodetic height. The system state variables are $\delta x = [\delta r^n \ \delta v^n \ \varepsilon^n \ \delta \omega^n \ \delta f^n]^T$. R_b^n is the transformation matrix from body frame to navigation frame. And w is system noise, the system noise matrix is expressed [14] as

$$G = \left[0_{9*1}, \sqrt{2\beta_{wx}\sigma_{wx}^2}, \sqrt{2\beta_{wy}\sigma_{wy}^2}, \sqrt{2\beta_{wz}\sigma_{wz}^2}, \sqrt{2\beta_{fx}\sigma_{fx}^2}, \sqrt{2\beta_{fy}\sigma_{fy}^2}, \sqrt{2\beta_{fz}\sigma_{fz}^2} \right]^T \quad (4)$$

where β_{wx}, β_{wy} and β_{wz} are the reciprocals of the correlation times of autocorrelation sequence of δ_{wx}, δ_{wy} and δ_{wz}; σ_{wx}, σ_{wy} and σ_{wz} are variance associated with gyroscope errors. β_{fx}, β_{fy} and β_{fz} are the reciprocals of the correlation times of autocorrelation sequence of δ_{fx}, δ_{fy} and δ_{fz}; σ_{fx}, σ_{fy} and σ_{fz} are variance associated with accelerometer errors.

3. PJ identification by fast orthogonal search

In **Figure 2**, the azimuth and pitch of PIG are invariant when it travels inside the SPS; they only changed at the PJ part. In addition, the roll of PIG is varied with the PIG rolling motion in the pipeline [15]. Therefore, the precise identification of the PJs between two adjacent SPSs could provide accurate azimuth and pitch updates indication for SINS in the corresponding SPS.

This section introduces a novel PJ detection technique by using FOS to analyze the MEMS accelerometer data. FOS is a random method that is used for the short-term signal processing, the time series analysis, and the complex system identification [16]. The simulated data sets are acquired when IMU is installed on the triaxial positioning and rate table at first. Then, the accelerometer data are analyzed and extracted by wavelet and FOS, respectively. After that, the detection result reveals the FOS could detect PJ from accelerometer data sets successfully when it is compared with the wavelet. Finally, FOS-based PJ detection result could provide indication for the azimuth and pitch updates in the corresponding SPS [16].

3.1. FOS-based PJ detection

3.1.1. Fast orthogonal search

FOS has been adopted in denoising and random error modeling of MEMS inertial sensors successfully [17]. An arbitrary set of nonorthogonal candidate function $p_m(n)$ is used to discover a functional expansion of an input $y(n)$ by minimizing the mean squared error (MSE) between $p_m(n)$ and $y(n)$ [18]. The input $y(n)$ in terms of the $p_m(n)$ is presented:

$$y(n) = \sum_{m=0}^{M} a_m p_m(n) + \varepsilon(n) \tag{5}$$

where $a_m (m = 1, 2,...,M)$ are the weights of $p_m(n)$, and $\varepsilon(n)$ is the model error.

The principle of FOS is to rediscover the right side of Eq. (5) into a sum of terms that are mutually orthogonal from $n = 0$ to N of the overall portion of the data:

$$y(n) = \sum_{m=0}^{M} g_m w_m(n) + e(n) \tag{6}$$

where $w_m(n) (m = 1, 2,...,M)$ denote the orthogonal functions that are generated from $p_m(n)$ by Gram-Schmidt orthogonalization method, which are yield by

$$w_m(n) = p_m(n) - \sum_{r=0}^{m-1} \alpha_{mr} w_r(n) \tag{7}$$

where

$$\alpha_{mr} = \sum_{n=0}^{N} p_m(n) w_r \left/ \sum_{n=0}^{N} (w_r(n))^2 \right. \tag{8}$$

$$g_m = \sum_{n=0}^{N} y(n) w_m(n) \left/ \sum_{n=0}^{N} (w_m(n))^2 \right. \tag{9}$$

The orthogonal expansion coefficients g_m are calculated to achieve a least-squares fitting:

$$MSE = \sum_{n=0}^{N} \left(y_n - \sum_{m=0}^{M} g_m w_m(n) \right)^2 \left/ (N+1) \right. \tag{10}$$

However, the construction of orthogonal expansion function $w_m(n)$ in Eq. (7) is high time and memory consumption. Here, the FOS computes the orthogonal expansion coefficients g_m without explicitly creating the orthogonal function $w_m(n)$ to significantly reduce the computing time and memory requirements consequently. The coefficients g_m are calculated by

$$g_m = C(m)/D(m,m), m = 0, \cdots, M \tag{11}$$

where

$$D(m,0) = 1, D(m,m) = \overline{p_m(n)}, D(m,r) = \overline{p_m(n)p_r(n)} - \sum_{i=0}^{r-1}\alpha_{mi}(m,i) \tag{12}$$

$$\alpha_{mr} = D(m,r)/D(r,r), m = 1, \cdots, M; r = 1, \cdots, m$$

with

$$C(0) = \overline{y(n)}; C(m) = \overline{y(n)p_m(n)} - \sum_{r=0}^{m-1}\alpha_{mr}C(r) \tag{13}$$

The MSE in Eq. (10) is equivalent to

$$MSE = \overline{y^2(n)} - \sum_{m=0}^{M}g_m^2 D(m,m) \tag{14}$$

The overbar of the previous equations is the time average that calculated over the portion of data recorded from $n = 0$ to N.

The MSE reduction given by math model addition is

$$Q_m = g_m^2\overline{w_m^2(n)} = g_m^2 D(m,m) \tag{15}$$

Therefore, FOS could search a model with a few fitting terms that reduce the MSE in order of its significance. Generally, FOS is terminated by one of the following three conditions. The first is when the predefined number of terms reached. The second is when the ratio of MSE to the mean squared value of the input signal is under a preset threshold. The third is when the reduction of the MSE by adding another term to the model is less than fitting the white Gaussian noise (WGN). FOS is completed by selecting the candidates $p_m(n)$ that are the pairs of sine and cosine functions at the interested frequencies. The candidate functions $p_m(n)$ are

$$\begin{cases} p_{2m-1}(n) = \sin(\omega_m n) \\ p_{2m}(n) = \cos(\omega_m n) \end{cases} \tag{16}$$

where $\omega_m(m = 1, 2,...,K)$ and K are the digital frequency and the number of the candidate frequency, respectively.

3.1.2. Design of FOS for PJ detection

In PJ detection, the accelerometer measurement data are transformed to a different domain by FOS to model the PIG motion dynamics from the inertial sensor measurement, and meanwhile to reject as much of the noises of inertial sensor as possible. In addition, the FOS extracts the singularity signals from the inertial sensors by its amplitude when maintaining the PJ detection precision.

The length of data record, the candidate functions, and the termination conditions could be used to determine the modeling accuracy of the FOS. The long-time recorded data are usually divided into a few short segments [19], and the each segment is modeled by FOS to extract the dynamic components from the noisy measurements. Furthermore, the frequency, amplitude, and phase of recorded data are included in the output of each segment of the FOS model terms, which could be utilized to synthesize an estimation of the true motion dynamics. Finally, all the segments are repeated by this process separately and recombined to implement the overall modeled data.

3.2. PJ detection implemented by FOS

3.2.1. Experimental equipment

Low-cost MEMS IMU Crossbow IMU300CC could measure the PIG triaxial angular rates and linear accelerations. Moreover, the Ideal Aerosmith 2103HT positioning and rate table are used to simulate the pipeline trajectory as shown in **Figure 2**. The experimental equipment of Crossbow IMU300CC, 2103HT table, table control panel, inertial sensors data acquisition system, and their corresponding connection are shown in **Figure 3**.

3.2.2. Experimental procedures

The simulated pipeline trajectory is similar to the one shown in **Figure 2**. The outer, middle, and inner table rotation axes are operated to accomplish the PIG attitude angles changes. Specifically, the rotation of table inner axis indicates that when PIG runs in the pipeline, it would experience varying degrees of rolling motion. The table middle axis could simulate the changes of pitch, and

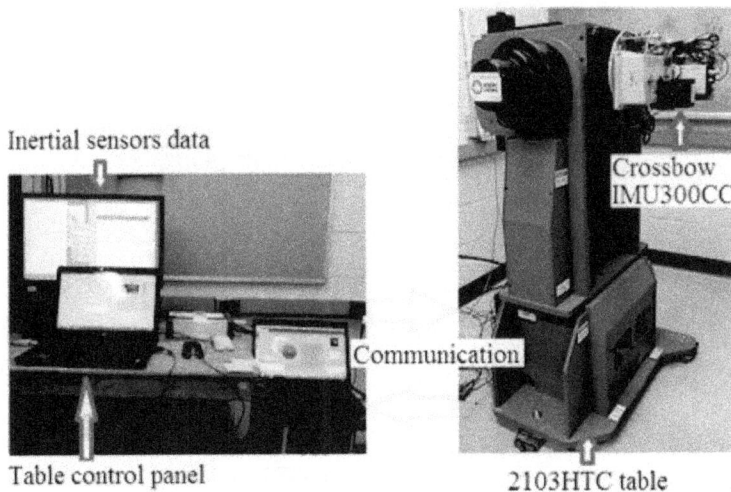

Figure 3. Crossbow IMU300CC and 2103HT table.

the PIG azimuth angle variations are simulated by table outer axis. The experiment is designed by as the following:

Firstly, the table rotates around the middle axis for 90° to make the PIG in horizontal plane as shown in right panel of **Figure 3**, which simulates the PIG launcher stage for pipeline inspection, and keeps this position for a few minutes to complete the initial alignment.

Secondly, the table middle axis rotates from horizontal position to −45°, which simulates the PIG movement from launcher to the underground pipeline.

Thirdly, the table middle axis rotates back to horizontal plane to simulate the starting of the regular PIG navigation stage.

Thirdly, rotate the outer axis every once in a while, to simulate the PIG runs in different pipeline segments with different azimuth angles.

Fourthly, move the table middle axis to 45°, which simulates the PIG movement from pipeline to receiver, then the middle axis rotates back to keep the PIG horizontal.

Finally, save and download the measurement data of inertial sensors, and the overall experiment period cost about 1700s.

3.2.3. Experimental result and discussion

Due to the rolling motion of PIG, the X-axis accelerometer in IMU is used for the data analysis, which is shown in **Figure 4**. The blue curve shows the raw X-axis accelerometer measurement

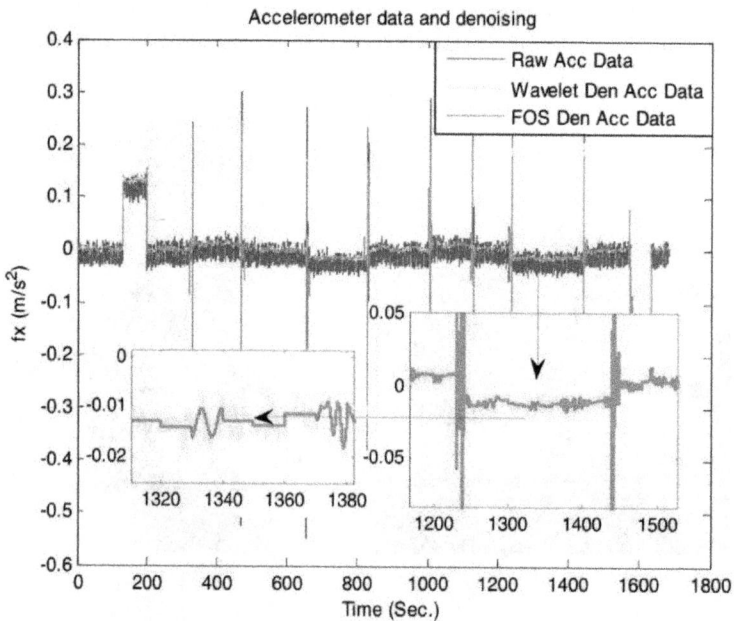

Figure 4. Raw accelerometer data (blue curve), wavelet denoised data (yellow curve), and FOS denoised data (red curve).

data that is contaminated by high Gaussian white noise (GWN). Hence, it is necessary to conduct data denoising before the PJ detection. The "db" family of wavelet was certificated to be a useful selection for the denoising of MEMS inertial sensors data [19]. Here, "db8" wavelet with four level of decomposition (LOD) is used for denoising on the accelerometer measurement data, and the result is demonstrated by yellow curve in **Figure 4**. In addition, FOS has shown superior performance in the denoising of low-cost MEMS inertial sensors in some applications [20], and the FOS denoised accelerometer data are represented by red curve in **Figure 4**. Both methods could provide robust MEMS accelerometer data denoising by reducing the random GWN level and maintaining the dynamic characteristic of the PIG. Moreover, FOS has shown significant improvement in the elimination of low-frequency noises, which could not be eliminated by wavelet denoising technology. Therefore, FOS is more suitable for low-cost MEMS inertial sensors for PJ detection application.

The upper panel in **Figure 5** reveals the raw measurement data of X-axis accelerometer. The jumps or spikes are the singular signals that expected to be identified accurately to provide azimuth and pitch updates in SPS. The lower panel of **Figure 5** also displays the amplitude that is calculated by FOS after the raw measurement data of accelerometer are denoised by FOS. The amplitude and the epochs indicate the singular signals of the raw measurement data of accelerometer.

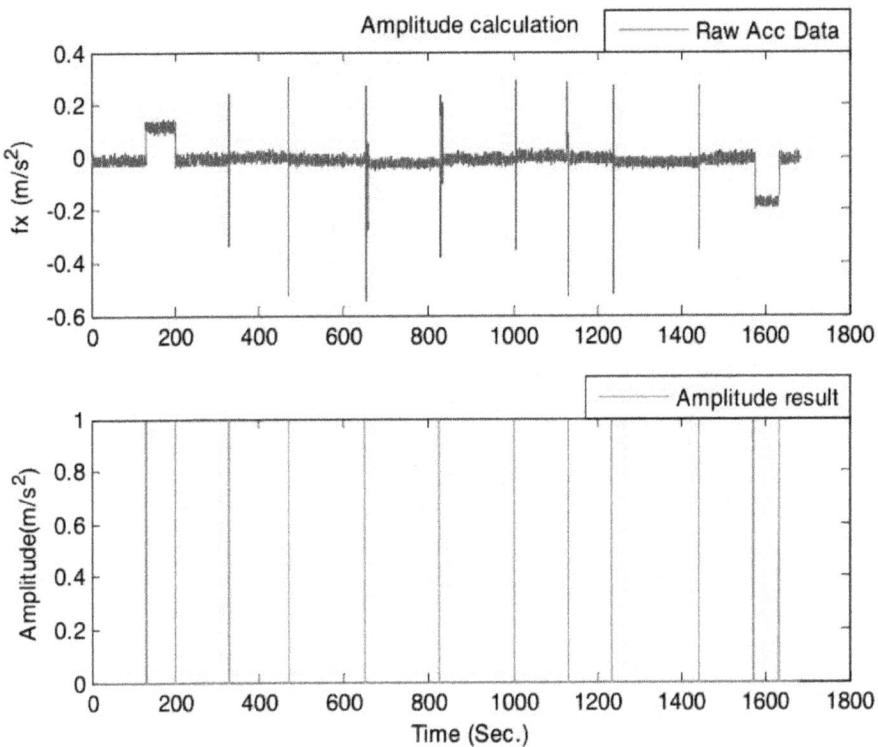

Figure 5. Raw X-axis accelerometer data (upper panel) and FOS amplitude (lower panel).

Figure 6 displays the PJ identification result by FOS on denoised measurement data of X-axis accelerometer. Specifically, the PIG passing through a PJ part is represented by the spike intervals in the red curve. These spikes are calculated by the preset threshold on the FOS amplitude. That is to say, when the FOS amplitude is bigger than the threshold, the intervals are detected as the PJs, while the other intervals are detected as SPSs. Furthermore, a magnified view of the second and third PJs in the **Figure 6** is also demonstrated to make the PJ detection result to be more intuitive. Specifically, a pitch angle variation of the PIG is shown by the second PJ, while an azimuth angle variation of the PIG is revealed by the third PJ. Therefore, the PJ could be detected correctly by FOS even with the raw accelerometer data in GWN-contaminated environment. After that, the accurate PJ detection results can be used for azimuth and pitch updates at the SPS in SINS.

The **Figures 4–6** shows the FOS-based PJ detection method on accelerometer measurement data for PIG navigation. The accelerometer measurement data are logged by using 2103HT table to simulate the azimuth and pitch changes of PIG in the pipeline. Moreover, the detection capability and precision of FOS are also verified with the FOS technology on accelerometer measurement data. The final results demonstrated that the FOS could detect the PJ correctly even when the accelerometer data contaminated with high GWN. Therefore, the proposed FOS can detect the PJ by measurement of the low-cost inertial sensors even in noised pipeline operational environments.

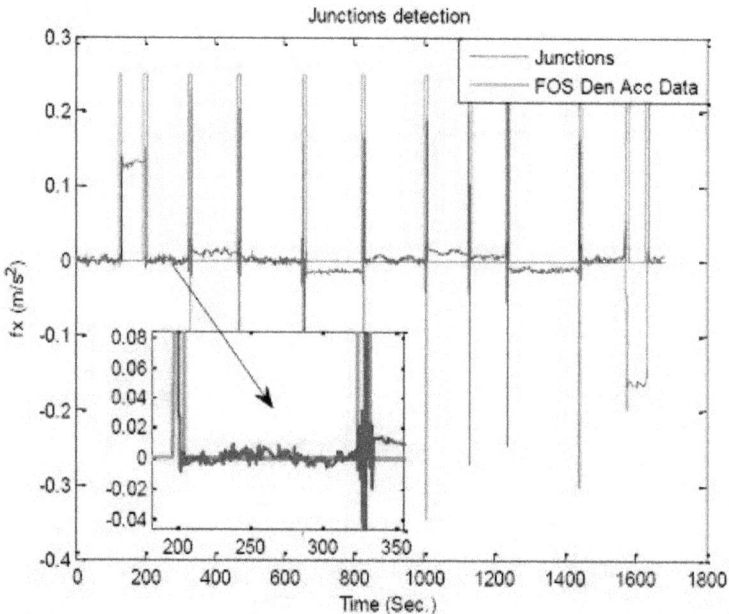

Figure 6. PJ recognition result by FOS.

4. MEMS SINS-enhanced PIG navigation system by PJ detection in small-diameter pipeline

In the above sections, the constant azimuth and pitch angles could be used to estimate the SINS errors in SPS. Therefore, this section would introduce an MEMS SINS-enhanced pipeline navigation system by PJ detection.

4.1. Introduction of micro-inertial/AGM/odometer/PJ system

Figure 7 shows the schematic diagram of the micro-inertial/AGM/odometer/PJ pipeline navigation system. The triaxial angular rate ω and triaxial linear acceleration f of PIG are measured by micro-inertial sensors in the pipeline. Then, the 3D attitude, velocity, and position of the PIG are provided by SINS mechanization. In order to correct the micro-inertial-sensor-error-induced PIG navigation error, the overall measurement updates include:

a. continuous azimuth and pitch updates in each SPS that are provided by PJ detection result,

b. 3D continuous velocity updates provided by odometers and PIG NHCs in pipeline, and

c. 3D sporadic coordinate updates provided by DGPS in the AGMs for every few kilometers.

Furthermore, these updates are both integrated by EKF and Rauch-Tung-Striebel smoother (RTSS) to estimate and correct the errors of micro-inertial sensors and the PIG navigation system [21].

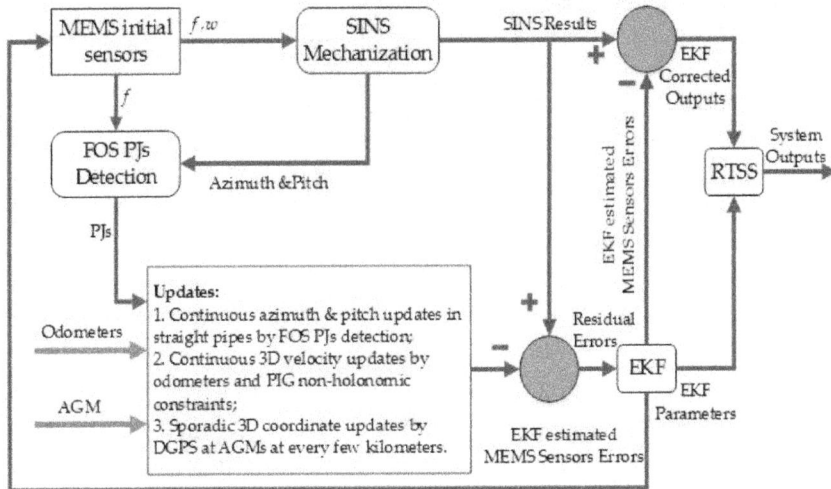

Figure 7. Schematic of micro-inertial/AGM/odometer/PJ-based pipeline navigation system.

4.2. Measurement models of micro-inertial/AGM/odometer/PJ system

The system error model is provided in Section 2.2. For the measurement state variables, there are four kinds of measurement models when PIG staying in different stages of the pipeline [22].

Firstly, when there are no AGMs in SPS, the measurement model of micro-inertial/odometer/PJ system is given by:

$$
\begin{bmatrix}
v_{e,m} - v_{e,SINS} \\
v_{n,m} - v_{n,SINS} \\
v_{u,m} - v_{u,SINS} \\
p_{PJ} - p_{SINS} \\
A_{PJ} - A_{SINS}
\end{bmatrix}
= H_1 \delta x -
\begin{bmatrix}
\delta\eta_{ve} \\
\delta\eta_{vn} \\
\delta\eta_{vu} \\
\delta\eta_p \\
\delta\eta_A
\end{bmatrix}
\tag{17}
$$

where $v_{e,m}$, $v_{n,m}$, and $v_{u,m}$ are the 3D velocity measurement updates from odometers and PIG NHCs. $v_{e,SINS}$, $v_{n,SINS}$ and $v_{u,SINS}$ are the 3D velocity calculated by SINS. $\delta\eta_{ve}$, $\delta\eta_{vn}$, and $\delta\eta_{vu}$ are the velocity measurement noise. p_{PJ} and A_{PJ} denote the pitch and azimuth angles that are calculated by SINS at the beginning of each SPS, respectively; $\delta\eta_p$ and $\delta\eta_A$ are the corresponding measurement noises. Therefore, the system measurement matrix H_1 is

$$
H_1 =
\begin{bmatrix}
O_{3*3} & I_{3*3} & O_{3*3} & O_{3*6} \\
O_{2*3} & O_{2*3} & H_{1,1} & O_{2*6}
\end{bmatrix}, H_{1,1} =
\begin{bmatrix}
1 & 0 & 0 \\
0 & 0 & 1
\end{bmatrix}
$$

Secondly, when there are AGMs in SPS, the system measurement model of micro-inertial/AGM/odometer/PJ is expressed as:

$$
\begin{bmatrix}
\varphi_{AGM} - \varphi_{SINS} \\
\lambda_{AGM} - \lambda_{SINS} \\
h_{AGM} - h_{SINS} \\
v_{e,m} - v_{e,SINS} \\
v_{n,m} - v_{n,SINS} \\
v_{u,m} - v_{u,SINS} \\
p_{PJ} - p_{SINS} \\
A_{PJ} - A_{SINS}
\end{bmatrix}
= H_2 \delta x -
\begin{bmatrix}
\delta\eta_\varphi \\
\delta\eta_\lambda \\
\delta\eta_h \\
\delta\eta_{ve} \\
\delta\eta_{vn} \\
\delta\eta_{vu} \\
\delta\eta_p \\
\delta\eta_A
\end{bmatrix}
\tag{18}
$$

where φ_{SINS}, λ_{SINS}, and h_{SINS} are the PIG position calculated by SINS mechanization. φ_{AGM}, λ_{AGM}, and h_{AGM} are the AGM position provided by DGPS. $\delta\eta_\varphi$, $\delta\eta_\lambda$, and $\delta\eta_h$ denote the AGM position measurement noise. Hence, the system measurement matrix H_2 is:

$$
H_2 =
\begin{bmatrix}
I_{6*6} & O_{6*3} & O_{6*6} \\
O_{2*6} & H_{2,1} & O_{2*6}
\end{bmatrix}, and\ H_{2,1} =
\begin{bmatrix}
1 & 0 & 0 \\
0 & 0 & 1
\end{bmatrix}.
$$

Thirdly, when there are no AGMs in PJ part, the system measurement model of micro-inertial/odometer is expressed as:

$$
\begin{bmatrix} v_{e,m} - v_{e,SINS} \\ v_{n,m} - v_{n,SINS} \\ v_{u,m} - v_{u,SINS} \end{bmatrix} = H_3 \delta x - \begin{bmatrix} \delta \eta_{ve} \\ \delta \eta_{vn} \\ \delta \eta_{vu} \end{bmatrix} \tag{19}
$$

and the system measurement matrix H_3 is:

$$
H_3 = \begin{bmatrix} O_{3*3} & I_{3*3} & O_{3*9} \end{bmatrix}.
$$

Fourthly, when there are AGMs in the PJ part, the system measurement model of micro-inertial/AGM/odometer is

$$
\begin{bmatrix} \varphi_{AGM} - \varphi_{SINS} \\ \lambda_{AGM} - \lambda_{SINS} \\ h_{AGM} - h_{SINS} \\ v_{e,m} - v_{e,SINS} \\ v_{n,m} - v_{e,SINS} \\ v_{u,m} - v_{n,SINS} \end{bmatrix} = H_4 \delta x - \begin{bmatrix} \delta \eta_{\varphi} \\ \delta \eta_{\lambda} \\ \delta \eta_{h} \\ \delta \eta_{ve} \\ \delta \eta_{vn} \\ \delta \eta_{vu} \end{bmatrix} \tag{20}
$$

The system measurement matrix H_4 is

$$
H_4 = \begin{bmatrix} I_{6*6} & O_{6*9} \end{bmatrix}
$$

During the measurement update stage of micro-inertial/AGM/odometer/PJ-based pipeline navigation system, the odometers and NHCs of PIG provide 3D continuous velocity updates, AGMs provide 3D sporadic coordinate updates, and PJ detection provides continuous azimuth and pitch updates in SPS. Therefore, when obtaining the EKF gain K_{Fk}, system states updates $\delta \hat{x}_{Fk}^+$ and system states covariance matrix P_{Fk}^+, the system design matrix H_k and the measurement covariance matrix R_k are calculated by the system measurement updates z_k when PIG in SPS or PJ part.

5. Experiments and results analysis

5.1. Experimental equipment

Husky A200 ™ robot (**Figure 8** left panel) from Clearpath Robotics of Canada is adopted to simulate the near-real situation of PIG running in an inspected pipeline. The pipeline-navigation-related sensors include VTI IMU, odometer, and so on. Specifically, two odometers are used in the left and right rear wheels of the robot for reducing the velocity measurement

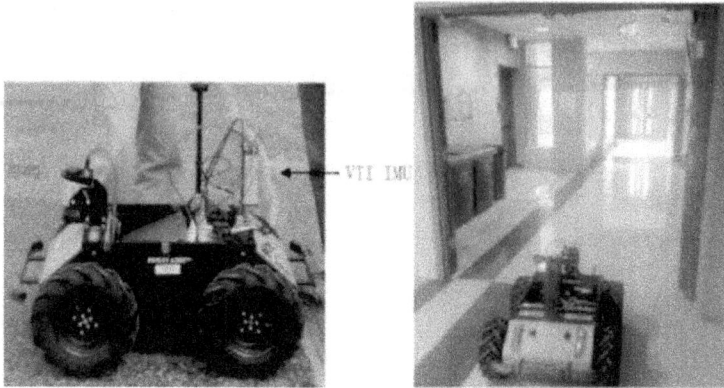

Figure 8. Husky A200™ robot and the experiment corridor.

error of micro-inertial sensors. In addition, the movement of this robot in straight line at the straight corridor can be controlled with remote controller, and the ground in the experiments is roughly horizontal (**Figure 8** right panel), which are adopted to simulate the NHCs and to eliminate the slippage of wheels of the PIG.

5.2. Experiment procedures

In the simulation experiment, Husky A200™ robot moves in a near rectangle corridor, which is around 70 m in length and 40 m in width. The detailed control parameters of Husky A200™ robot are set as following:

a. The forward velocity of the Husky A200™ robot is near 1 m/s, and it moves in a fixed direction in each straight corridor, which simulates the PIG running in straight pipeline.

b. The robot turns 90° at the end point of each straight corridor and, meanwhile, to keep the robot running, which is used to simulate the PIG go through the bend pipeline.

c. In each long and straight corridor, the protrusion is preset at every 5–10 m to simulate the movement of PIG over the circular weld or the flange.

d. The overall length of the experiment in each closed circle is about 220 m, and only the coordinates of start point and final point are used as coordinate updates.

In addition, the whole experiment is conducted within indoor and seven landmarks are derived from the coordinates measured by DGPS from roof corners of the experimental building to be set as referenced landmarks.

Figure 9 displays seven red landmarks at some corners of the rectangular corridor, which are derived by the seven yellow circle coordinates at the roof corners of the experimental building. Moreover, the starting point or final point of the experiment is shown on the upper right position of the floor map by a star symbol.

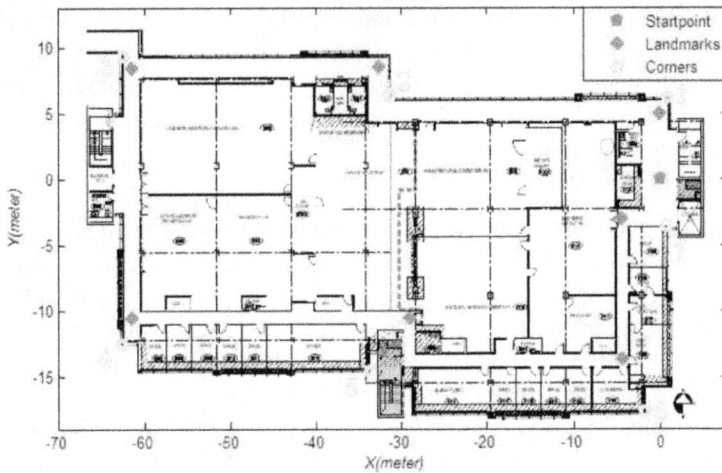

Figure 9. The landmarks for the experiment in corridor.

5.3. Experimental results and analysis

5.3.1. Pipeline junction detection

In **Figure 10**, the PJ detection result is obtained by Z-axis accelerometer measurement data of VTI IMU with FOS. The blue and red signals denote the raw and denoised accelerometer measurement data, respectively. The difference between the blue and red signals not only revealed the feasibility of FOS denoising on VTI IMU, but also demonstrated that the

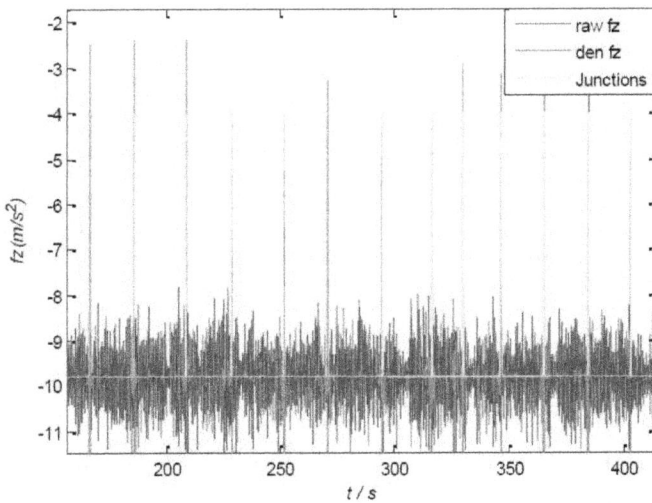

Figure 10. The PJ detection results by FOS.

signal-to-noise ratio of accelerometer measurement data could be improved greatly. In addition, the yellow curve in **Figure 10** is the PJ detection results; the spike intervals display that the Husky A200™ robot is passing a 90° corridor or a preset protrusion, while the rest of the intervals represents the robot going through the straight corridor segment.

5.3.2. EKF- and RTSS-estimated results

The EKF-estimated PIG navigation system result is shown in **Figure 11** by the blue trajectory. It only utilizes the forward velocity provided by the odometers and also the PIG NHCs updates to reduce the system error. The maximum position error of the blue trajectory is 18.93 m in the eighth landmark, and meanwhile, the corresponding mean error is 10.86 m. Meanwhile, the azimuth and pitch errors correction in each SPS of the PIG navigation system is provided by the PJ detection result. And the EKF/PJ-estimated PIG navigation system is shown in **Figure 11** with yellow trajectory. The maximum position error of yellow trajectory is 8.75 m in the eighth landmark, and the corresponding mean error is 4.96 m. So, the mean error of PIG navigation system improves 54.328% at all eight landmarks after adding the azimuth and pitch errors correction by EKF/PJ estimation. However, the position precision of EKF estimation technique on micro-inertial sensors still cannot fulfill the precision requirements of PIG navigation system when the azimuth and pitch errors correction are added in SPS. Fortunately, the RTSS offline estimation technology can be used to improve the position precision of the PIG navigation system once after the EKF estimated result.

In **Figure 12**, the blue curve denotes the trajectory of EKF- and RTSS-estimated PIG navigation system with 3D continuous velocity error and 3D coordinate correction at the starting point. The maximum position error of blue trajectory at the fifth landmark is 6.62 m, and the corresponding mean error is 3.73 m. In addition, the PJ-identified azimuth and pitch errors correction at the SPS is also utilized to improve the position precision of PIG navigation

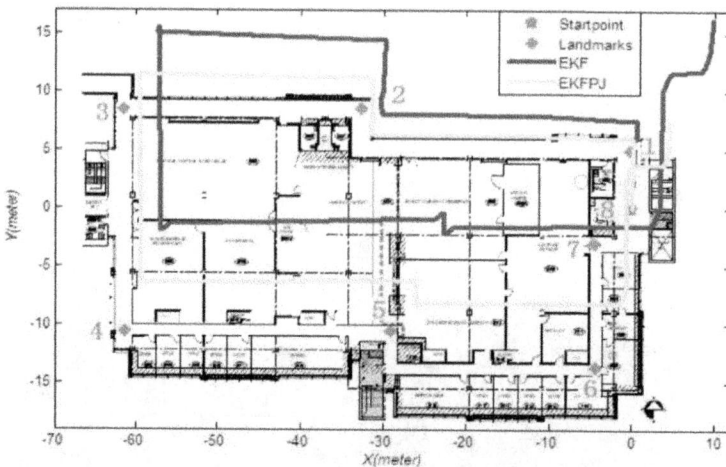

Figure 11. The trajectories of EKF-estimated PIG navigation system.

system. The yellow trajectory is the result of the EKF/PJ/RTSS-estimated PIG navigation system. The maximum position error of blue trajectory is 3.08 m at the fifth landmark, and the corresponding mean error is 1.70 m. Therefore, the mean error of PIG navigation system at the overall eight landmarks improves 54.42% after adding azimuth and pitch errors correction with EKF/RTSS estimation technology.

Subsequently, the statistic results of PIG navigation system errors at all eight landmarks that are optimized by EKF, EKF/PJ, EKF/RTSS, and EKF/PJ/RTSS are listed in **Table 1**. Specifically, the second column is position errors of PIG navigation system estimated by EKF when it is compared with the referenced eight landmarks. The position errors are increased with the PIG traveling distance from 1.96 m at first landmark to 18.93 m at last landmark. Then, the third

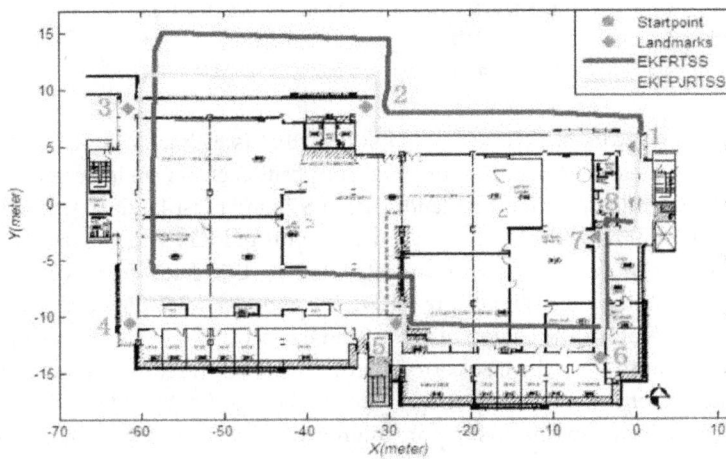

Figure 12. The trajectories of EKF/RTSS-estimated PIG navigation system.

Landmarks	EKF	EKF/PJ	EKF/RTSS	EKF/PJ/RTSS
1 (m)	1.96	0.76	1.98	1.01
2 (m)	5.77	2.53	2.77	1.28
3 (m)	8.06	3.81	4.14	1.75
4 (m)	10.03	4.74	5.73	2.76
5 (m)	11.39	5.08	6.62	3.08
6 (m)	14.53	6.59	6.24	2.78
7 (m)	16.19	7.44	2.37	0.93
8 (m)	18.93	8.75	0	0
Max (m)	18.93	8.75	6.62	3.08
Mean (m)	10.86	4.96	3.73	1.7

Table 1. The statistic result of PIG navigation system error.

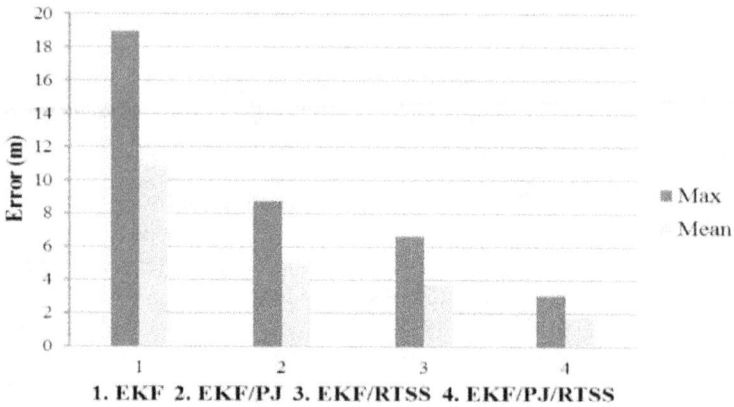

Figure 13. The errors of PIG navigation system by various optimization methods.

column is position errors of PIG navigation system that is estimated by EKF/PJ when it is compared with the referenced eight landmarks. The position errors are increased with the PIG traveling distance from 0.76 m at first landmark to 8.75 m at last landmark. In addition, the fourth and fifth columns of **Table 1** denote position errors of PIG navigation system when it is referenced to all eight landmarks that are estimated by EKF/RTSS and EKF/RTSS/PJ techniques. The maximum errors estimated by EKF/RTSS and EKF/RTSS/PJ are 6.62 and 3.08 m at the fifth landmark that has the longest distance from the start point or coordinate update point. This is mainly because of the inverse correction by RTSS, which reduces the position error of PIG navigation system when the trajectory is close to the coordinate update points. Therefore, both the maximum error and mean error are improved by the RTSS estimation technique.

More intuitively, both the maximum and mean errors of the PIG navigation system estimated by EKF, EKF/PJ, EKF/RTSS, and EKF/PJ/RTSS are shown by column chart in **Figure 13**. Both maximum and mean errors are improved greatly when adding the PJ detection result and the RTSS estimation technique.

6. Conclusions

This chapter presents a micro-inertial-aided high-precision positioning method for small-diameter PIG navigation, which is based on the micro-inertial/AGM/odometer/PJ PIG navigation system. Apart from the previous 3D continuous velocity updates from odometers and NHCs and the 3D sporadic coordinate updates from AGMs, the proposed micro-inertial/AGM/odometer/PJ-based PIG navigation system also adds continuous azimuth and pitch error correction in each SPS to reduce the divergent SINS-error-induced PIG navigation error. Furthermore, an indoor-Husky-robot-simulated PIG experiment is implemented to testify the performance of the PJ detection result on PIG navigation system, and the mean error of PIG navigation system improved 54.42% after adding azimuth and pitch errors correction by EKF/RTSS estimation technique.

Acknowledgements

This work was sponsored by the National Natural Science Foundation of China (61803118), the Science and Technology Research Program of Chongqing Municipal Education Commission (KJZD-K201804701), the Post Doc. Foundation of Heilongjiang Province (LBH-Z17053) and the Fundamental Research Funds for the Central Universities (HEUCFJ180402).

Author details

Lianwu Guan[1]*, Xu Xu[1], Yanbin Gao[1], Fanming Liu[1], Hanxiao Rong[1], Meng Wang[1] and Aboelmagd Noureldin[2]

*Address all correspondence to: guanlianwu@hrbeu.edu.cn

1 College of Automation, Harbin Engineering University, Harbin, China

2 Department of Electrical and Computer Engineering, Queen's University, Kingston, Canada

References

[1] Coramik M, Ege Y. Discontinuity inspection in pipelines: A comparison review[J]. Measurement. 2017;**111**:359-373. DOI: 10.1016/j.measurement.2017.07.058

[2] Available from: https://cepa.com/en/ [Accessed: 29-06-2016]

[3] Ben Y, Yang J, Yin D, Li Q. System reset of strapdown INS for pipeline inspection gauge. Ocean Engineering. 2014;**88**:357-365. DOI: 10.1016/j.oceaneng.2014.07.004

[4] Gloria NBS, Areiza MCL, Miranda IVJ, Rebello JMA. Development of a magnetic sensor for detection and sizing of internal pipeline corrosion defects. NDT and E International. 2009;**42**(8):669-677. DOI: 10.1016/j.ndteint.2009.06.009

[5] Wenman T, Dim JC. Pipeline integrity management. In: ICPTT 2011@Sustainable Solutions for Water, Sewer, Gas, and Oil Pipelines. ASCE; 2012. pp. 1532-1540. DOI: 10.2118/ 161948-MS

[6] Liu Z, Kleiner Y. State of the art review of the inspection technologies for condition assessment of water pipes. Measurement. 2013;**46**:1-15. DOI: 10.1016/j.measurement.2012.05.032

[7] Gao Y, Guan L, Wang T. Optimal artificial fish swarm algorithm for the field calibration on marine navigation. Measurement. 2014;**50**:297-304. DOI: 10.1016/j.measurement.2014.01.003

[8] Martell HE. Applications of strapdown inertial systems in curvature detection problems. International Hepatology Communications. 1991;**3**(95):147-147. DOI: 10.5072/PRISM/18281

[9] Guan L, Gao Y, Osman A, et al. Analysis of rolling motion effect on SINS error modeling in PIG, IEEE/ION position, location and navigation symposium (PLANS). Savannah, GA: IEEE; 2016. pp. 681-686. DOI: 10.1109/PLANS.2016.7479761

[10] Guan L, Gao Y, Osman A, et al. Pipeline junction detection from accelerometer measurement using fast orthogonal search, position, location and navigation symposium. IEEE. 2016:21-26. DOI: 10.1109/PLANS.2016.7479678

[11] Sahli H, Moussa A, Noureldin A, et al. Small pipeline trajectory estimation using MEMS based IMU. In: Proceedings of the 27th International Technical Meeting of The Satellite Division of the Institute of Navigation (ION GNSS+ 2014); September 2014; Tampa, Florida. pp. 154-161

[12] Kok M, Schön TB. Maximum likelihood calibration of a magnetometer using inertial sensors. IFAC Proceedings Volumes. 2014;**47**(3):92-97. DOI: 10.3182/20140824-6-ZA-1003.02025

[13] Hanna PL. Strapdown inertial systems for pipeline navigation. In: Inertial Navigation Sensor Development, IEE Colloquium on IET. 2002. pp. 7/1-7/3

[14] Noureldin A, Karamat TB, Georgy J. Fundamentals of Inertial Navigation, Satellite-based Positioning and their Integration. Springer Berlin Heidelberg; 2013. DOI: 10.1007/978-3-642-30466-8

[15] Ernst HK. The rolling pig or how does a survey creep through a pipeline. Bulletin Geodesique. 1994;**68**(2):71-76. DOI: 10.1007/BF00819383

[16] Korenberg MJ, Paarmann LD. Orthogonal approaches to time-series analysis and system identification. IEEE Signal Processing Magazine. 1991;**8**(3):29-43. DOI: 10.1109/79.127999

[17] Chon KH. Accurate identification of periodic oscillations buried in white or colored noise using fast orthogonal search. IEEE Transaction on Biomedical Engineering. 2001;**48**(6): 622-629. DOI: 10.1109/10.923780

[18] Shen Z, Georgy J, Korenberg MJ, Noureldin A. Nonlinear modeling and identification of inertial errors with application to 2D vehicle navigation. In: Proceedings of the 22nd International Technical Meeting of The Satellite Division of the Institute of Navigation (ION GNSS 2009), International Journal of Navigation and Observation; New York, USA. 2009. pp. 593-599

[19] Noureldin A, Armstrong J, El-Shafie A, et al. Accuracy enhancement of inertial sensors utilizing high resolution spectral analysis. Sensors. 2012;**12**(9):11638-11660. DOI: 10.3390/s120911638

[20] Shen Z, Georgy J, Korenberg M, Noureldin A. FOS-based modeling of reduced inertial sensor system errors for 2D vehicular navigation. Electronics Letters. 2010;**46**:298-299. DOI: 10.1049/el.2010.2507

[21] Chowdhury MS, Abdelhafez MF. Pipeline inspection gauge position estimation using inertial measurement unit, odometer, and a set of reference stations. Sensors and Actuators B: Chemical. 2016;**2**(3):234-243. DOI: 10.1115/1.4030945

[22] Guan L, Cong X, Sun Y, et al. Enhanced MEMS SINS aided pipeline surveying system by pipeline junction detection in small diameter pipeline[J]. IFAC-PapersOnLine. 2017; **50**(1):3560-3565. DOI: 10.1016/j.ifacol.2017.08.962

Chapter 5

Optimization of NOE Flights Sensors and Their Integration

Tamilselvam Nallusamy and Prasanalakshmi Balaji

Additional information is available at the end of the chapter

http://dx.doi.org/10.5772/intechopen.86139

Abstract

This chapter unveils an enhancement strategy for nap-of-the-earth. The nap-of-the-earth (NOE) mode is the most energizing, most unsafe, and is generally the slowest. Military aircraft to maintain a strategic distance from opponent detection and assault in a high-thread circumstance use it. NOE used to limit discovery by the ground-based radar, targets and the control system. The radar altimeter (RA) or terrain following radar (TFR), terrain awareness and warning system (TAWS) used to identify the curbs during flying in NOE flights. Here, while the plane is at the nap of the earth activity, the speed and the height must be moderate as effectively decided. The terrain following radar (TFR) keeps up the altitude from the beginning. Therefore, we analyze the issue to expand the performance of the airplane by extending the terrain by a few modes of the TAWS, which given by various aviation authorities[1]. Further to this, different TAWS modes of action, explanation of mode selection and progression in TAWS clarified in detail. This chapter displays the MATLAB programme for a few patterns of TAWS mission, and simulation of the flight path for the excessive terrain closure rate from mode two operation of the flight.

Keywords: nap-of-the-earth, radar system, MATLAB programming, terrain awareness and warning system

1. Introduction

Nap-of-the-earth (NOE) is a very low-altitude flight route utilized by military plane to keep away from enemy detection and assault in the high-threat environment. This mode is the slowest

---

[1] International civil aviation organization (ICAO), United Kingdom civil aviation (UKCA), civil aviation authority (CAA) and federal aviation authority (FAA)

IntechOpen

© 2019 The Author(s). Licensee IntechOpen. This chapter is distributed under the terms of the Creative Commons Attribution License (http://creativecommons.org/licenses/by/3.0), which permits unrestricted use, distribution, and reproduction in any medium, provided the original work is properly cited. (cc) BY

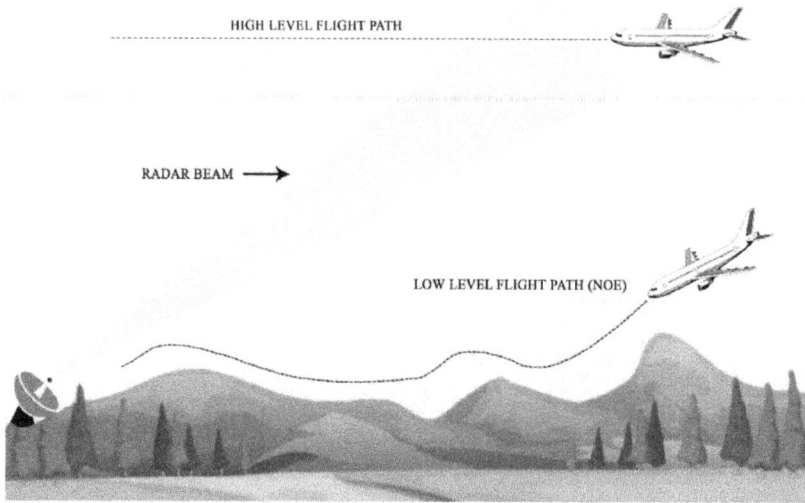

Figure 1. Nap-of-the-earth flight.

but exciting. When flying at the nap of the earth, the pilot flies at varying airspeed, altitude, and remains as close to the earth's floor as feasible. Geographical functions used during NOE flight, and this keeps below enemy radar coverage [1]. NOE used to reduce detection through an antagonistic plane, ground-based radar, or onslaught targets. Doppler radar can decide NOE flight, but the aircraft that comes closer to has to be inside radar range within the first area, and low flight minimizes this opportunity because of the impact of terrain protecting [2].

The lowest NOE flying is by helicopters because they have lower speeds and more maneuverability than fixed-wing aircraft, mainly in the fast-jets. Only helicopters can fly at treetop levels or even below height of surrounding trees where there are clear areas (such as in river gullies), flying under wires (such as electricity cables). Attack helicopters can hide behind trees or buildings, popping up just enough to use their (rotor mast-mounted) radar or other sensors and then minimally exposing themselves to launch weapons. Then further NOE flying can make the escape [2].

Figure 1 represents the nap of the earth operation. In this, the high-level route and the low-degree route of the flight served. The high-level path identified by using the radar device from the base, while the low-level flight direction used to fly below the radar. They have their flight course, which avoids the collision with terrain.

2. Sensors in NOE flights

In most case, pilots perform the NOE operation in daylight hours using visual reference. The commonly used navigation systems are:

1. Radar altimeter.

2. Terrain-following radar system.

3. Terrain awareness and warning system.

In this chapter, TAWS modes given by the ICAO analyzed. The global positioning system (GPS) also helps to find the exact position of the flight from the decision height (DH).

3. Obstacle detection and analysis

There are two types of obstacle detection in NOE flights:

1. Detection using active sensors.

2. Detection using passive sensors.

3.1. Obstacle detection using passive sensors

A passive sensor is a microwave device developed to collect and measure natural emissions produced by components of the earth's surface and its ecosystem [2, 3]. The passive sensor measures the output as a combination of environmental temperature, surface roughness, surface composition, and other physical properties. The measurements of passive sensors determined with the help of molecular resonance by fixing the radio frequency bands. These frequencies no longer alternate and statistics could not duplicate in other frequency bands. The passive sensors could able to detect low-quality emissions particularly very sensitive multitude emissions on the ground both from the frequency band wherein measurements made and from out-of-band. Spaceborne passive sensors offer the capacity to acquire all-climate, day and night, worldwide observations of the earth and its environment [2, 3].

3.2. Obstacle detection using active sensors

An active sensor measures the signals that reflected, refracted or scattered from the earth's surface or its atmosphere. Spaceborne active sensors worked on the radar principle and used in many applications related to atmospherelogy, meteorology [2]. For example, Doppler radar analyses the electromagnetic echo from a moving object and define the absolute velocity of the object; mapping radars use synthetic aperture radar to scan the sizeable geographical area for geography. There are some specific radar systems to identify the human density in the forest as well as the construction area by measuring the reflective waves. Navigation radars commonly employed in ships for collision avoidance and it works by sensing reflections. Spaceborne active sensors used in the meteorological-satellite communication services. Sensor frequency allocations recurrently shared with supplementary radar systems; as such, systems frequently well matched with the operation of the sensors [2, 3].

4. Radar altimeter

The radio altimeter does not depend on radar standards beyond the way that it reacts to reflected signs. The radio altimeter used to show targets roughly around 300 miles. The time gap between the transmitted and received signals analyzed by radar altimeter and that determined the distance between the destinations. A radio altimeter communicates an FM tweaked continuous wave 4 GHz signal. Their frequency balanced on "entrance ramp" with the goal that it changes direction. The spectrum between the transmitted and received signals ceaselessly analyzed to show altitude above the terrain [2, 4]. The radio altimeter does not depend on radar standards beyond the way that it reacts to reflected signs. It used to show targets roughly 300 miles. The time gap between the transmitted and received signals analyzed by radar altimeter and determined the distance between the destinations. A radio altimeter communicates an FM tweaked continuous wave 4 GHz signal. Their frequency balanced on "entrance ramp" with the goal that it changes direction. The spectrum between the transmitted and received messages ceaselessly analyzed to show altitude above the terrain radar altimeter essentially projected to display the target locations within 2500 feet. It is inactive when the aircraft fly above 2500 feet [2]. A typical radio altimeter system on an airplane utilizes two antennas namely transmitting and receiving antenna. The transmitting and receiving antennas arranged as close to the point of the hinge as could expect under the circumstances, generally under the fuselage between the wings. Positioning and installation of the antenna in flight vehicle is very critical and harsh work. The antenna should never be situated at the nose or tail because the angle of attack could then contribute genuine mistakes [2, 5]. Low altitude flying airplanes use radio altimeter technology for escaping from ground radar detection. This technology is very famous in military based flying vehicles like helicopters. Terrain-following radar also uses this technology for allowing a plane to fly at high speeds over varied topography [1].

4.1. Working principle and applications

Radar altimeter works on one of the two methods. They are,

1. pulse modulated radar and

2. frequency modulated continuous wave FMCW radar.

4.1.1. Pulse modulated radar

Pulse modulated radar consists of a series of discrete pulsed radiation. In this method, the distance between the targets identified by analyzing the reflected transmitted radio waves.

4.1.2. Frequency modulated continuous wave (FM-CW) radar

Frequency modulated continuous wave radar (FM-CW) is capable of determining distance and is a short-range measuring radar set. This increases the reliability of the system. When more than one reflected wave arrives at the radar antenna, providing distance measurement along with speed measurement is essential for identification. This kind of radar used to measure the exact height during the landing procedure of aircraft. It also used as early-warning radar and proximity sensors. The difference in frequency between that received from the ground and that transmitted is a measure of the time delay [2, 6, 7].

4.2. Applications of radar altimeter

4.2.1. Civil applications of radar altimeter

Radar altimeters frequently used by business aircraft for landing, particularly in low-visibility situations and in automatic landings by enabling the autopilot to sense when to begin the flare maneuver. Radar altimeters transfer information to the autothrottle. Above ground level (AGL), radar altimeters commonly give interpretations up to 2.5 K feet (760 m). The automatic landing capability of today's airplanes enhanced by installing at least one or usually several radar altimeters. Concorde and the British Aircraft Corporation BAC, 1–11 were equipped with radar altimeters even though they are old aircraft. In the present day, some of the smaller airplanes in a sub-50 seater category like jet stream series and ATR 42 are using radar altimeter [2, 6, 7].

4.2.2. Military applications

Military airplane utilizes radar altimeters to fly relatively very nearer to ground and the ocean to avoid radar detection. These radar altimeters are very much useful while targeting anti-aircraft weapons or surface-to-air missiles. Radar altimeter also used in terrain following radar. TFR allows fighter-bombers to fly at very low altitudes through radar altimeter system. In the advanced combat aircrafts, forward terrain looking radars used [6, 7].

5. Terrain following radar

Terrain-following radar is an aviation innovation that permits an extremely low-flying airplane to keep up a moderately constant height over the ground level. It dependent on TAWS and called as ground-hugging or terrain-hugging flight. It is like a GPWS. Record the general objectives of a TFR system in two classifications. The first of these would be to minimize detection by the opponent; subsequently, it is a vital factor or else the mission will fall flat if the aircraft identified. TFR provides active radar avoidance by increasing the terrain mask, lowering the altitude, lowering the RF signature, escaping or reducing the time in threat coverage and operation at night and adverse weather condition [4, 8, 9].

Minimizing detection is of no use if the flight crash inbound or outbound on the mission. Therefore, the other primary goal of a TFR is to offer maximum flight safety. Flight safety maximization achieved by maintaining safe altitude from terrain, avoiding unpredicted obstacles, consistent performance of the system, high availability/reliability [4, 8, 9].

The major goals of terrain following radar represented in **Figure 2**, the risk vs. terrain average clearance plotted in the graphical form. It helps us to determine the total risk value. This total

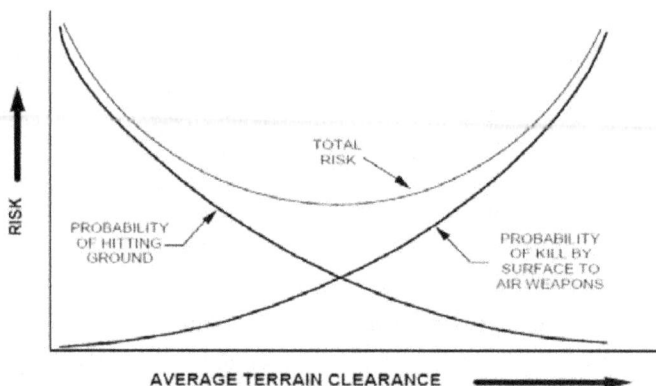

Figure 2. Terrain following radar vs. risk [4].

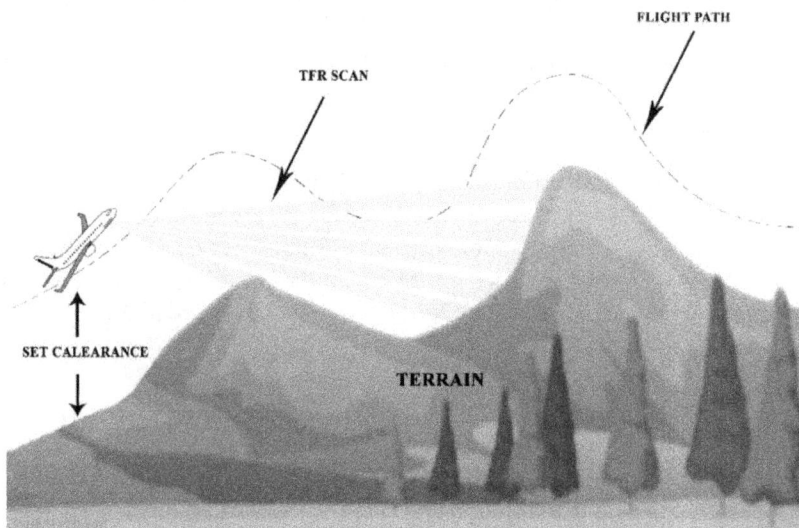

Figure 3. Terrain following radar scan.

risk obtained by the ground hitting probability and the probability of kill by the weapons, which varies in the order with risk and terrain clearance plot [4, 8, 9].

5.1. Scanning of terrain following radar

Terrain following radar scans the air gap in front of aircraft with a vertical scan. It produces a wedge of information in vertical, horizontal and azimuth direction. TFR scan the plane by referring horizon as the middle and provide the wedge above, below, left side, right side facet. All wedge patterns ware interpreted and analyzed. An antenna scan pattern to produce this wedge illustrated in **Figure 3**.

5.2. Algorithm of terrain following radar

There have been several approaches to the terrain-following algorithms. The typical algorithm of terrain following radar is shown in **Figure 4a–d** which represents the following algorithms. They are,

1. template algorithm,

2. angle algorithm,

3. advanced low altitude algorithm, and

4. path following algorithm.

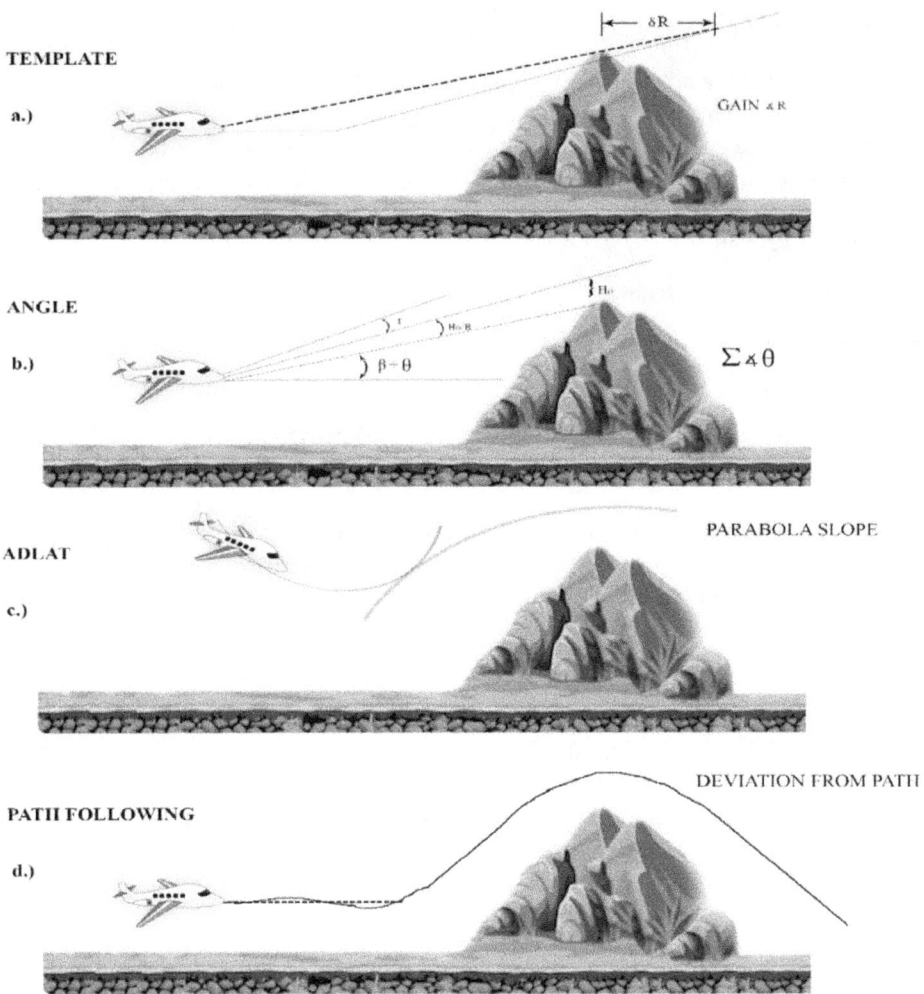

Figure 4. (a, b, c, and d) Terrain following radar computation approaches.

5.2.1. Template algorithm

Template algorithm creates two virtual lines in front of the aircraft in the airspace. These virtual lines form two sections; the upper one is decided based on the pitch up maneuvering of the airplane, whereas the lower part anticipated the set clearance. The terrains monitored as the radar scans the airspace in front of the aircraft. The return signals collected and processed for storing range and angle to the region. A pull up command generated when the terrain or other object crosses the template line. On the other hand, when the terrain clears the template line, a pulldown command generated. This full down command, bring the aircraft to original set clearance decided by the pilot [4]. This system implemented using analog processing prior to the advent of digital circuitry. **Figure 4a** shows the template algorithm.

5.2.2. Angle algorithm

Angle algorithm is the advanced version of template algorithm because it developed from the template algorithm. Similar to the template algorithm, the lower line set as the desired set clearance of the aircraft. Angle algorithm uses some of the angles, which displayed in **Figure 4b**. For clear understanding, one should know about the following terms:

- β—antenna scan angle
- θ—pitch angle of the aircraft
- Ho—desired set clearance
- R—range to the point of interest
- Γ—margin factor to allow for the pushover point at the peak of the climb not to drop below the set clearance.

When these angles combined, one will get the perspective to the object. For smaller angles, the total angle can be approximated by Ho/R. The margin factor tuned to the response of the aircraft. Further development in angle algorithm carried out, but coverage range minimized [4, 8, 9].

5.2.3. Advanced low altitude algorithm

Advanced low altitude or ADLAT algorithm developed at the start of the digital computation age. The concept of the ADLAT algorithm is to construct a parabola where the derivative taken to give a zero slope at the peak of the climb at the desired set clearance. Computation of this algorithm processed through individual terrain points and consistently updated as the airplane approaches maximum. To solve parabolic flight path related calculations, ADLAT algorithm uses square root functions and complex formulae. **Figure 4c** shows the probable flight path developed through parabolic derivative. From **Figure 4c**, it is clear that the offset terrain path defines the set clearance. Flying over a terrain, aircraft tend to surpass the preferred set clearance because aircraft could not make direct flight direction changes and equal the offset path [4, 8, 9].

5.2.4. Path following algorithm

Path-following algorithm is an advanced concept than all other algorithms because it requires significant computation power. In this method, a path developed by the flight when moving over terrain with the offset being the set clearance. Path-following algorithm generates flight path by tracking and correcting the offsets as the plane travels over the region. The path-following algorithm shown in **Figure 4d** [4, 8, 9].

6. Terrain awareness and warning system

Terrain awareness and warning system (TAWS) is a piece of airborne safety equipment designed to provide a warning on terrain collision to the pilot reliably and automatically [10]. Ground proximity warning system (GPWS) is the universally accepted system and developed from TAWS [15, 16].

TAWS provides proper warning about the upcoming obstacles and terrains by using terrain database and GPS positioning. Since TAWS depend on terrain database and GPS positioning, it gives a prediction based upon projected location and aircraft location. The system warns pilots by providing both voice and visual intimations. The pilot takes action according to the warning received from TAWS [11, 12]. The system is time-dependent, and therefore it reimburses the performance of aircraft and speed. TAWS and GPWS are not same because TAWS produces warning signals based on the aircraft's real position (indicated by built-in GPS) concerning a terrain map installed in the equipment whereas GPWS produces warnings only through the inputs received from the radio altimeter [15, 16].

TAWS works by using the instrumental values (like inbuilt GPS) and digital elevation data of the aircraft to know the future position, which interconnects the ground. So the pilot intimated through audio warning and visual warning about the upcoming terrain well in advance. **Figure 5** shows the typical TAWS (right side). The image, which displayed in the left side, shows different colors for the respective altitude rate from sea level by reference altitude [10–12].

6.1. There are mainly three classes in the terrain awareness and warning system

They are TAWS class A, TAWS class B and TAWS class C.

TAWS Class A provides the following features:

- Forward looking terrain avoidance (FLTA) by taking account of terrain, aircraft to generate alerts of both ahead and below the reduced terrain clearance and warnings of the terrain impact.

- A terrain awareness display, which shows terrain above the aircraft current altitude and up to 2000 feet below it, which can provide proactive situational awareness as well as safety net, functions.

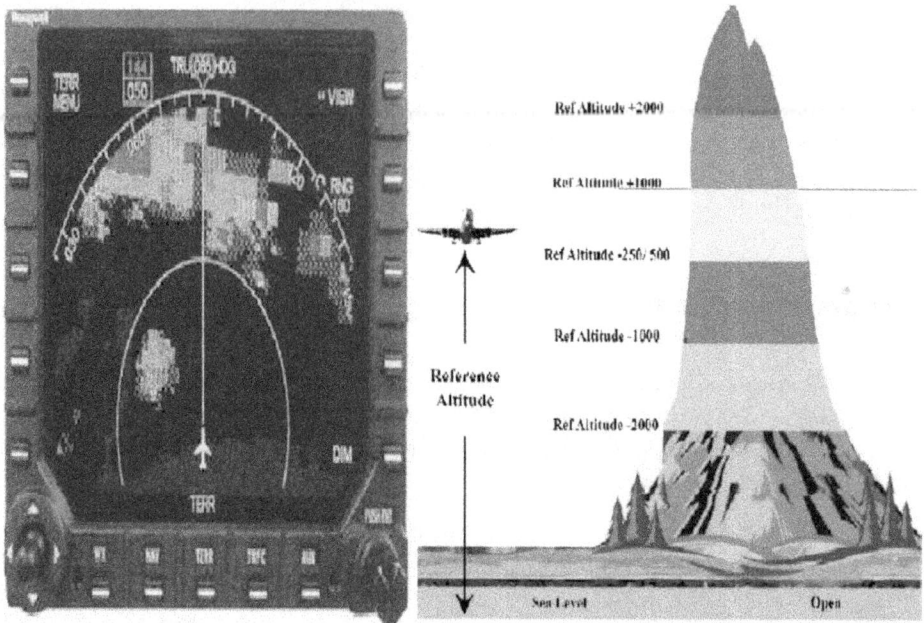

Figure 5. Terrain awareness and warning system.

- Basic GPWS functions—modes 1–6 using radio altimeter input moderated by aircraft position in relation to database terrain and obstacles (note that the mode 6 requirement is altitude voice call out(s).

- Premature descent alerting (PDA) if the aircraft descends below a normal approach path for the nearest runway.

TAWS Class B equipment provides the following:

- Forward looking terrain avoidance by taking account of terrain, the aircraft to generate alerts of reduced terrain both ahead of and below clearance and warnings of terrain impact.

- Basic GPWS modes 1, 3 and 6 only (there is no radio altimeter input).

- Premature descent alerting if the aircraft descends below a normal approach path for the nearest runway.

6.2. Modes of operation

The various sets of hazardous conditions that the GPWS monitors and provides alerts for commonly referred to as modes. These described in detail in the following paragraphs. Hazard awareness provided by TAWS aural alerts or warnings and illumination of alert and warning lights in response to different situations. **Table 1** shown below illustrates a typical TAWS system mode of the operation of flight, respectively.

6.3. Response to a TAWS activation

TAWS is a safety system, which provides two different warning when aircraft approaches terrain namely soft warning and hard warning. Soft warning indicates an unusual status with respect to terrain location that needs immediate attention and a change in aircraft configuration or flight path. On the other hand, hard warning indicates an unsafe situation, which needs immediate action. TAWS response procedures appropriately designed by operator based on the flight type and performance [13, 14].

6.4. Problem description

MATLAB program for the TAWS mode and its descriptions presented in this chapter. The **"Excessive terrain closure rate"** determination for **mode 2** programmed and simulated. The program created by using altitude-measuring formula by considering arbitrary pressure values for the various altitude

$$Z = \left(\frac{-RT}{gM}\right) ln P_0 - ln P \tag{1}$$

where Z—height from the ground, RT—gas constant temperature, g—gravity, P_0—random pressure value, P—sea level pressure, respectively.

The ultimate aim of the program is to fly the aircraft in the well-defined path without collision. For example, for the mode operation set the "z" value for some extent. When it detects some obstacles, i.e., in excessive terrain closure rate, it will show **"TERRAINTERRAIN" "PULL UP"** message and when it comes to normal steady flight shows **"NO WARNING"** message.

Mode	Condition	Aural alert	Aural warning
1	Excessive descent rate	"SINKRATE"	"PULL UP"
2	Excessive terrain closure rate	"TERRAIN TERRAIN"	"PULL UP"
3	Excessive attitude loss after take-off or go around	"DON'T SINK"	(NO WARNING)
4a	Unsafe terrain clearance while gear not locked down	"TOO LOW GEAR"	"TOO LOW TERRAIN"
4b	Unsafe terrain clearance while landing flap not selected	"TOO LOW FLAP"	"TOO LOW TERRAIN"
4c	Terrain rising faster than aircraft after take off	"TOO LOW TERRAIN"	(NO WARNING)
5	Excessive descent below ILS glideslope	"GLIDESLOPE"	"GLIDESLOPE"(1)
6a	Advisory callout of radio height	(for example) "ONE THOUSAND"	(NO WARNING)
6b	Advisory callout of bank angle	"BANK ANGLE"	(NO WARNING)
7	Wind shear protection	"WINDSHEAR"	(NO WARNING)
NOT MODE NUMBERED	Terrain proximity	"CAUTION TERRAIN"	"TERRAIN TERRAIN PULL UP"

Table 1. The modes of operation in TAWS [17].

6.5. MAT LAB programing

6.5.1. Program for mode 2 "Excessive terrain closure rate"

Here, at the mode 2 operation, if the "z" value more than 2500 feet, the display will show "NO WARNING" message. When the height drops 2500 feet and below, TAWS will show TERRAIN message and if reduced to 1500 feet, PULL UP message will show.

INPUT DATA

clear all; clc;

%% Definition of input pressure

P = 1e3.*[75.232 70 60 50 65 75 80 76 60 65 70 75 80 84 89 80 76 70 65 60 55]'; %% Initialization of other required parameters

Rsp = 287; %(J/(kg /(kg K)) specific gas constant for air

T = 298; %(kelvin) assuming constant temperature throughout altitude Pnot = 101.325e3; %(Pa) sea-level pressure

g = 9.81 ;%(ms^-2) acceleration due to gravity %z(size(P))=[];

% %Calculation of height and display of message for i = 1: size (P)

z(i) = (Rsp*T/g)*log(Pnot/P(i));

if (z(i) >= 2500) disp('NO WARNING') elseif (z(i) >= 1500) disp('TERAINTERRAIN') else disp('PULL UP') end

end

%%Note

%z = 2500 corresponds to P = 75.232 kPa %z = 1 500corresponds to P = 84.748 kPa %z = 0000 corresponds to P = 101.325 kPa

6.5.2. Program for the simulation of excessive closure rate

In this simulation of excessive closure rate, we are going to simulate the aircraft moving on its path without collision with the terrain using the terrain awareness and warning system (mode 2) as per the regulation. The mode 2 warns flight crew of excessive closure rates with the rapidly rising terrain. If terrain rises significantly within 2000 feet of the aircraft, the terrain closure rate is measured. Up to this stage the "NO WARNING" message is displayed and when the aircraft reaches the maximum closure value at the higher threat condition the "TERRAIN TERRAIN PULL UP" message is displayed. And when the aircraft passes the terrain it came to normal low level fight and then "NO WARNING" message is shown.

INPUT DATA

%#control animation speed DELAY =0.1;num =1000; num1=500 %# create data x =linspace(-pi,pi,num); c =linspace(-4,-pi,num1) e =linspace(pi,6,num1) y=(sin(x+1.5))

s=(sin(x+1.5))+1.5d=zeros(1,num1) for k=1:num1 d(1,k) = 0.5

end

f=zeros(1,num1) for l=1:num1 f(1,l) = 0.5 end

%# plot graph

plot(x,y,x,s,c,d,e,f),xlabel('x'), ylabel('y'), title('Flight Path'),grid on %# create moving point + coords text

hLine = line('XData',x(1), 'YData',s(1), 'Color','r', ...

'Marker','^', 'MarkerSize',15, 'LineWidth',2);

hTxt = text(x(1), s(1), sprintf('(%.3f,%.3f)',x(1),y(1)), ...

'Color','r', 'FontSize',10, ...

'HorizontalAlignment','left', 'VerticalAlignment','top');

hLine1 = line('XData',c(1), 'YData',d(1), 'Color','r', ...

'Marker','^', 'MarkerSize',15, 'LineWidth',2);

hTxt1 = text(c(1), d(1), sprintf('(%.3f,%.3f)',c(1),d(1)), ...

'Color','r', 'FontSize',10, ...

'HorizontalAlignment','left', 'VerticalAlignment','top');

hLine2 = line('XData',e(1), 'YData',f(1), 'Color','r', ...

'Marker','^', 'MarkerSize',15, 'LineWidth',2);

hTxt2 = text(e(1), f(1), sprintf('(%.3f,%.3f)',e(1),f(1)), ...

'Color','r', 'FontSize',10, ...

'HorizontalAlignment','left', 'VerticalAlignment','top');

for j=1:length(c)

disp('WARNING!! TERRAIN TERRAIN PULL UP!!') set(hLine1, 'XData',c(j), 'YData',d(j))

set(hTxt1, 'Position',[c(j) d(j)], ...

'String',sprintf('(%.3f,%.3f)',[c(j)d])) drawnow

j= rem(j+1,num1)+1;

if ~ishandle(hLine), end end

fori=1:length(x) set(hLine, 'XData',x(i), 'YData',s(i)) set(hTxt, 'Position',[x(i) s(i)], ...

'String',sprintf('(%.3f,%.3f)',[x(i) s(i)]))

drawnow

i = rem(i+1,num)+1; if ~ishandle(hLine), end end

```
for n=1:length(e) disp('NO WARNING')
set(hLine2, 'XData',e(n), 'YData',f(n)) set(hTxt2, 'Position',[e(n) f(n)], ...
'String',sprintf('(%.3f,%.3f)',[e(n) f(n)])) draw now
n= rem(n+1,num1)+1; if ~ishandle(hLine2),
end end
```

7. Conclusion

This chapter presented the optimization method for nap-of-the-earth flight operation using the sensors. In the nap of the earth operation, if we took in to the deep look, the use of terrain awareness and warning system has drastically decreased the collision with ground or the obstacles, which occurred while on controlled flight. However, with the advanced technological improvements and modern equipment, the accidents of collision are still happening.

The establishment of new systems and improving the existing ones may lead to prevent the accidents while flying at nap of the earth operation or at the low-level flying. Hence, the proper training to the pilot is mandatory to fly at the low altitude level with using the advanced equipment. Here in this project the terrain awareness and warning system taken for the safe flight operation. Further to this, different TAWS modes of operation and the explanation of mode selection in TAWS explained in detail. The MATLAB programming done for one mode of TAWS operation, the simulation of flight path for the excessive terrain closure rate from the mode 2 operation of flight is determined, and the outputs gained for the nap of the earth flights.

Acknowledgements

The authors are grateful to Mangalore Institute of Technology and Engineering, Mangalore, India and King Khalid University, Abha, KSA.

Author details

Tamilselvam Nallusamy[1]* and Prasanalakshmi Balaji[2]

*Address all correspondence to: selva.gte.research@gmail.com

1 Department of Aeronautical Engineering, Mangalore Institute of Technology and Engineering, Mangalore, Karnataka, India

2 Department of Computer Science, King Khalid University, Abha, KSA

References

[1] Anon. Helicopters at War (Blitz Editions). 1st ed. UK: Bookmart Ltd; 1996. ISBN-9781856053457

[2] Tamilselvam N, Divya Priya D, Rajeswari B, Siddika N. Navigation systems. Noe flight sensors and their integration. ARPN Journal of Engineering and Applied Sciences. 2016;**11**(2):1285-1292. Available from: http://www.arpnjournals.org/jeas/research_papers/rp_2016/jeas_0116_3493.pdf

[3] Thuy M. NASA Directorates. What are Passive and Active Sensors? National Aeronautics and Space Administration; 2012. Available from: https://www.nasa.gov/directorates/heo/scan/communications/outreach/funfacts/txt_passive_active.html [Accessed: 2017]

[4] IEEE. Proceedings of the IEEE 1979 National Aerospace and Electronics Conference NAECON 1979; Part III, 1979; New York, NY, USA1979. pp. 1089-1096. Available from: http://www.theatlas.org/index.php?...a-history-of-terrain-following-radar

[5] Bhanu B, Das S, Roberts B, Duncan D. System for Obstacle Detection During Rotorcraft Low Altitude Flight. July 1996. Available from: http://www.researchgate.net/publication/3002633 [Accessed: August 1996] DOI: 10.1109/7.532250A

[6] Jim L. Types of radar. Improved forms of radar. In: Frequency Modulated Continuous Wave Radar. Scotland: University of St. Andrews. 2001. Available from: https://www.st-andrews.ac.uk/~www_pa/Scots_Guide/RadCom/part15/page2.html [Accessed: 2019]

[7] Ahmad B. Radar/Radio 2013 Flight Instruments & Radio Navigational Aids-Radar/Radio Altimeter. 2013. Available from: http://www.slideshare.net/sajid93/radar-altimeter-assignment?Next_slideshow=1 [Accessed: November 2013]

[8] Starling RJ, Stewart CM. The development of terrain following radar. Aircraft Engineering & Aerospace Technology Journal. 1971;**43**(4):13-15. DOI: 10.1108/eb034756

[9] Krachmalnick FM, Vetsch GJ, Wendl MJ. Automatic flight control system for automatic terrain following. Journal of Aircraft. 1968;**5**(2):168-175. DOI: 10.2514/3.43925

[10] Paul N. Terrain Awareness and Warning Systems—TAWS. Pilots Guide. 2005. Available from: https://www.skybrary.aero/bookshelf/books/2328.pdf

[11] Duncan Aviation. Straight Talk About TAWS (Terrain Avoidance and Warning System). 2002. Available from: www.duncanaviation.aero/files/straighttalk/Straight_Talk-TAWS.pdf

[12] Technical Standard Order—Terrain Avoidance and Warning System. 2002. Available from: http://www51.honeywell.com/aero/common/.../TSOC151bPaper.pdf

[13] EASA. CS-ETSO/Amendment 2-Change Information. 2005. Available from: https://easa.europa.eu/system/files/dfu/NPA_14_2005.pdf

[14] Federal Aviation Administration. 14 CFR Parts 91, 121, 135. 1995. Available from: http://www.faa.gov/documentlibrary/media/Advisory_Circular/AC_23-18.pdf [Accessed: 17 December 2002]

[15] Terrain Awareness and Warning System Modes of Operation. 2014. Available from: http://www.skybrary.aero/index.php/Terrain_Avoidance_and_Warning_System_%28TAWS%29

[16] United Kingdom Civil Aviation Authority. Ground Proximity Warning Systems. Specification No. 14. Issue: 2. 1976. Available from: www.caa.co.uk/docs/33/CASPEC14.PDF [Accessed: September 2002]

[17] https://skybrary.aero/index.php/Terrain_Avoidance_and_Warning_System_(TAWS), 2014

www.ingramcontent.com/pod-product-compliance
Lightning Source LLC
Chambersburg PA
CBHW081234190326
41458CB00016B/5780

* 9 7 8 1 8 3 8 8 0 5 6 4 7 *